Children and Political Violence

Understanding Children's Worlds

General Editor Judy Dunn

The study of children's development can have a profound influence on how children are brought up, cared for, and educated. The central aim of this series is to encourage developmental psychologists to set out the findings and the implications of their research for others – teachers, doctors, social workers, students – who are responsible for caring for and teaching children and their families. It aims not to offer simple prescriptive advice to other professionals, but to make important innovative research accessible to them.

How Children Think and Learn
David Wood

Children and Emotion
Paul L. Harris

Making Decisions about Children
Psychological Questions and Answers
H. Rudolph Schaffer

Bullying at School
What we know and what we can do
Dan Olweus

Children and Political Violence
Ed Cairns

Children and Political Violence

Ed Cairns

First published 1996
2 4 6 8 10 9 7 5 3 1

Blackwell Publishers Ltd
108 Cowley Road
Oxford OX4 1JF
UK

Blackwell Publishers Inc
238 Main Street
Cambridge, Massachusetts 02142
USA

British Library Cataloguing in Publication Data
A CIP catalogue record for this book is available from the British Library.

Library of Congress Cataloging-in-Publication Data
Cairns, Ed.
Children and political violence / Ed Cairns.
p. cm. — (Understanding children's worlds)
Includes bibliographical references and index.
ISBN 1–55786–350–4 (hardbound : alk. paper). — ISBN 1–55786–351–2 (pbk. : alk. paper)
1. Children and war. 2. Children and violence. 3. Child psychology. 4.Violence—Psychological aspects. I. Title. II. Series.
HQ784.W3C37 1996
305.23—dc20 95–12471
CIP

Typeset in Sabon on 11/13 pt by CentraCet Limited, Cambridge
Printed in Great Britain

This book is printed on acid-free paper.

For
Ali and Reem,
and all victims of
political violence

Contents

Series Editor's Preface

There has been an extraordinary neglect of the topic of the impact of political violence on children's development and well-being. All over the world, children are witnessing, experiencing and participating in acts of violence perpetrated by one set of people upon another: in the Middle East, the US, the Far East, Bosnia, Northern Ireland, India and South America. Yet the effects of such violence on children's adjustment and relationships, their social identity, aggression, moral sensibility, and political understanding are little understood. Clearly political violence could influence children in a wide variety of ways, for instance through an increase in the economic problems faced by the children's families. In this book it is the psychological and social impact of the violence on children that is the chief focus. Dr Cairns concentrates primarily on the small but growing body of systematic, quantitative studies that are available. In bringing together these scattered studies – many of which are little known to a wide audience – he provides a notably timely and important discussion of what is known, what needs to be known, the pitfalls and limitations of the research, and how these might be overcome.

He examines the nature of stress and coping in children faced by political violence; considers the direct and indirect impact of such violence on children's daily lives; and explores the nature of children's involvement in political violence, children as political activists and insurgents themselves. His concern with quantitative research means that he draws chiefly on studies from South Africa, Israel, The Lebanon and Northern Ireland, but he is always sensitive to the patchy nature of the available information and significance of the particular political contexts of the situations studied. The findings raise many theoretical points of general importance, for instance the possibility that the effects of political violence may be caused indirectly by poverty, or by separation from family. The poignant examples cited bring the drama and terror of these children's experiences vividly alive to us. Clarifying the developmental implications of children's experiences, including the experience of political violence that is all too common and widespread, is a key goal of the series *Understanding Children's Worlds* in which this book appears.

Acknowledgements

I would like to thank a number of people who have helped me, either directly or indirectly, to produce this book including the series editor and an anonymous reviewer. In particular I am grateful to Michael Roe who was kind enough to read an earlier version of the manuscript and comment on it in detail – despite the fact that he was on sabbatical at the time!

He, along with many other friends from around the world, especially at the Psychology Department, University of Cape Town and the International Conflict Resolution Centre at the University of Melbourne, plus countless undergraduates and many loyal graduate students, have listened to various earlier versions of much of what is written here.

Closer to home I would like to thank others such as the staff of the Library at the Coleraine campus of the University of Ulster (in particular those working in the Inter-library Loans Office), as well as Betty Hempill and Pat Short for their many kindnesses.

As ever my gratitude and love goes to my family, especially my wife who had to bear the brunt of family life on her own while I was locked in the garden shed.

Ed Cairns

1 Introduction

Background

With the whole world embroiled in war, a conference was held at the White House, in January 1940, and a report 'Children in a Democracy' subsequently published. Shortly after, a child psychologist, Despert (1942), reviewing the proceedings, reported that she found the study to be 'disappointing' in so far as psychological considerations were concerned, with only one short chapter, 'The Child in the Family', dealing with children's emotional needs (Despert, 1942, p. 33). Why was this? There is nothing new about political violence. For centuries children have been exposed to its dangers in one form or another. The history of many countries is a long recitation of wars. On this subject millions upon millions of words have been written. Reading such history books, however, one gets the impression that the world of political violence is largely a world of adults, indeed a world of adult men.

Until relatively recently women, and children in particular, have been invisible socially and therefore irrelevant to, and apparently immune from, the great events of the world's nations (Burman, 1986). This is partly, no doubt, a legacy of the fact that until a few hundred years ago virtually all western societies did not really think of children as full members of society or even, some would claim, as proper human beings (Hareven, 1986). Even in this century it has been claimed that in the history of the Holocaust 'children are conspicuously, glaringly, screamingly, silently absent' (Dwork, 1991, p. 253).

Whatever the reason, today it is becoming harder for those who chart the social impact of wars to concentrate only on the participants at the sharp end and to ignore civilians completely. It is becoming harder because today civilians are increasingly becoming the target of war. This is easily seen from a glance at the casualty statistics: World War I recorded 10 per cent civilian casualties; World War II some 50 per cent. However, in all subsequent wars around 80 per cent of casualties have been civilians (Dodge, 1990). Or to put it another way – the ratio of soldiers to civilians killed in armed conflict has shifted from approximately 9:1 in the early decades of this century to 1:9 in recent conflicts such as Lebanon (Garbarino et al., 1991b). Obviously it is difficult to say how many of these casualties have been children but a common estimate is that during the 1980s alone some 1.5 million children may have died while an additional 4 million may have been injured (Lederer, 1994). Further, even more children (perhaps as many as 15 million) may have managed to escape physically but still have had their lives thrown into turmoil as they and their families fled to other countries or became 'internally displaced' within their own countries (Committee on Labor and Human Resources, U.S. Congress, 1990).

This dearth of information on children and war is not due simply to the fact that the two disciplines which might have been expected to take the lead in such an area of study – psychiatry and psychology – are relatively new sciences. In fact this century has seen the accumulation of a great deal of research dealing with military psychiatry. Despite this, research on the effects of war on civilians is scant. One is therefore forced to conclude that civilian mental health is obviously not thought to be as important for a nation to succeed. Rather societies at war prefer to direct most of their professional resources toward catering for the well-being and efficiency of their fighting soldiers (Punamaki, 1987).

Punamaki (1987, p. 15) has also suggested another explanation for this imbalance in the research profile. This is, that in the peculiar human and ideological atmosphere of a society at war 'psychological disturbances are easily interpreted as signs of weakness' . A society at war, she suggests, cannot afford to let the enemy know about their citizens, possible psychic suffering and lack of endurance. Therefore, war propaganda seeks to create an image of the citizens as brave and heroic and hence seeks to avoid research which might contradict this stance.

One other possible explanation for the meagre amount of research in this area is that researchers are intimidated by the ethical problems of research on children in war-time (this topic will be dealt with more fully later in the chapter). This relates to the fact that social scientists of all hues, and especially psychologists, claim scientific neutrality. This has not been seen as a stumbling block for psychological investigation where children are caught up in an all-out war. However in societies such as South Africa (Liddell and Kvalsvig, 1990), and Northern Ireland (Cairns, 1987), ethical issues and the question of neutrality have proved to be more problematic.

Whatever the reasons why psychologists and others have neglected the topic of children and political violence in the past, today the need for a higher research profile for this area is greater than ever. In particular, the world must be made to realize that the connection between 'the long war on poverty and underdevelopment', and 'a more equitable international order remain fundamental determinants of children's survival, health and well-being' (UNICEF, 1984, p. 16). This, as recent devastating famines have shown, is particularly important in Africa where children account for nearly half the population and are the most vulnerable along with their mothers and grandparents in war-time (Dodge, 1990).

Despite such problems individual researchers, often, but not always, psychologists or psychiatrists, have begun to try to understand the impact of political violence on children. In the main, these researchers are focusing on questions relating to the impact of political violence on such things as children's aggression, moral development, and interpersonal relations. Others are concerned with children who witness, experience or participate in violent acts and the effects of war or combat on the social fabric of children's lives, including loss of families, destruction of social networks, hunger, and homelessness. Some of these same researchers are also studying children's stress and coping in violent circumstances, and the impact of specific interventions on their psychological well-being. Often these researchers are motivated by the need to put themselves in a better position to offer advice on psychological 'first aid', while for many there is also the hope that something will be learned, which will prevent the transmission of attitudes and values, endemic in political violence, to succeeding generations.

Even a cursory review of the academic literature reveals, however, that such researchers are thin on the ground, especially in the Third World. As a result, each researcher is almost always working in isolation without financial backing. Given these circumstances, it is not surprising that, to date, their work has not made a major impact on mainstream academia.

What is available is a very small corpus of research, often published in local journals or books, which is totally lacking in cross-cultural or comparative efforts. As a result researchers in many parts of the world appear to think that the problems faced by children in their society are peculiar to that society alone, presumably because they are unaware of similar work done elsewhere.

None of this explains why research is needed which focuses specifically on children and political violence. In the US alone, thousands of children suffer annually either as the victims of violence or because they witness violent events. For example, Novello (1991) reports that in a public housing development in Chicago virtually all of the children under 5 years had had a first-hand encounter with a shooting. Similarly Pynoos and Eth (1985, p. 21) have estimated that children in Los Angeles witness 10–20 per cent of homicides. As they point out, if this applies to the whole of the US then several thousand children per year witness a murder – often of one of their parents. In addition, according to these authors, children also witness such things as rape (including of course marital rape) and parental suicide. Finally, children are themselves often the victims of various forms of domestic violence.

With thousands of children per year suffering because they are exposed to all this violence, in a country which has more psychologists per head of population than any other in history, why is it necessary to study the impact of political violence on children here – a type of violence which occurs more frequently in the poorer countries of the world where psychologists are thin on the ground?

Perhaps the most obvious reason is that political violence (as noted earlier) has the potential to affect many more children than does criminal or domestic violence. Further, what evidence there is appears to suggest that this is a problem that is likely to get worse not better.

The principal reason, however, that research is often carried out in this area is that adults believe that political violence has the potential to be more stressful for children than other forms of violence. For example, psychologists and psychiatrists in England at the beginning of the 'Blitz' in the early 1940s felt that it was inevitable that air raids would 'lead to widespread panic and hysteria' (Vernon, 1941) with psychiatric casualties possibly exceeding physical casualties by three to one. This belief was so widespread that the government committee given the task of dealing with civilians in London at first suggested not evacuation when the air war began, but rather that a police cordon be thrown around London in order to prevent the 'disorderly and general flight' which they anticipated (Titmus, 1950). In fact, when the Blitz got underway the problem was sometimes persuading people to leave, not stopping them from fleeing.

Also, the reason why political violence is thought by some to be potentially more stressful is because of its 'concealed, unresolved and cumulative' nature (Punamaki, 1987). According to Punamaki the prolonged nature of political violence and its unpredictability also makes it especially likely to be more psychologically damaging. In fact, as the evidence reviewed in chapter 2 will show, for various reasons children may actually be remarkably more resilient than adults have believed.

More recently researchers have come to realize that political violence should be studied not just because it can damage children directly, but also because it can have a more far-reaching impact on society as a whole and therefore may impact indirectly in more subtle ways on the everyday lives of children. This is a theme that will be developed in chapter 3.

Yet another reason for studying the impact of political violence on children is that it may hold clues to ways of ensuring that political violence will not be perpetuated. This topic will be taken up again in chapters 4 and 5.

There are also solid academic reasons to carry out research in this area. Research on children exposed to political violence can contribute to knowledge in the area of developmental psychology generally, by allowing us to test the generality of theories and hypotheses, which have originated, for example, in relation to the impact of criminal or domestic violence on children.

This is possible because political violence is in essence so completely different from criminal or domestic violence. The difference arises because the latter involves interpersonal violence, while political violence involves intergroup violence. Intergroup violence ultimately still means confrontations between individuals, but now the individuals behave violently because of their group affiliation. This in turn means that intergroup violence (unlike most interpersonal violence) is much more likely to involve people who are strangers to each other (Hoffman and McKendrick, 1990) and its consequences are likely to be more far-reaching. As Ayalon (1983, p. 296) has noted, 'The hostility that individuals encounter in their daily lives in the modern civilized world is seldom expressed as the intention to annihilate them utterly in cold blood, or to obliterate their humanity by reducing them to worthless objects.'

For these various reasons it can be argued that the impact of political violence on children merits special attention. In particular, the distinction between interpersonal and intergroup conflict is, in my opinion, a key one which, taken in relation to the role of social identity in settings of political violence, will inform discussion of various issues throughout this book.

This distinction between interpersonal and intergroup conflict stems originally from the work of Tajfel (1981) on social identity theory. Social identity theory came about because of dissatisfaction with earlier attempts on the part of social psychologists to explain intergroup conflict. The main criticism of the earlier theories was that they tended to see intergroup conflict and intergroup attitudes as primarily the property of individuals and also that they tended to see intergroup conflict and hence political violence as a form of irrationality. Social identity theory takes a diametrically opposed position by suggesting that there is a fundamental difference between interpersonal and intergroup processes. It follows, therefore, that intergroup processes cannot be explained by resorting to interpersonal processes.

According to Tajfel's original theory we tend to divide our social world into social categories, and inevitably see ourselves as belonging to certain types of social categories, but not to others. In this way, the theory claims, we tend to develop various social identities. That is we come to conceive of ourselves in terms of 'the defining features of a set of a self-inclusive social category that renders self stereotypically "interchangeable" with other in-group members and stereotypically distinct from outgroup members' (Hogg, 1992, p. 90).

These two processes, social categorization and the formation of social identities are, according to Tajfel (1978, p. 50), critical links in the development of intergroup conflict because as Tajfel has pointed out

> in order for large numbers of individuals to be able to hate or dislike or discriminate against other individuals seen as belonging to a common social category they first have acquired a sense of belonging to groups (or social categories) which are clearly distinct from and stand in certain relations to those they hate, dislike or discriminate against.

Whether our behaviour will be determined by our social identity or by our personal identity will depend upon the particular psychological situation. The theory proposes that all interactions fall along a continuum which stretches from interpersonal interaction at one end to social interaction at the other. The closer the situation is to the social end of the continuum the more our behaviour is determined by our group membership and in such situations people are more likely to see themselves as exemplars of the in-group and to see each other as exemplars of the out-group.

Social identity theory also suggests that not only do we divide the world into social groups and develop a social identity associated with these groups but also that we are motivated to enhance our feeling about ourselves, and one way of doing this is to make sure that our social identity is positively evaluated. This we do by making comparisons between those social groups and other social groups with which we identify in an attempt to ensure that our group achieves social psychological distinctiveness.

According to the theory these processes become particularly crucial in situations where, because of history or social structure, it is not possible to leave a group that is not contributing to the positive evaluation of self. In such situations, where two major groups predominate and where the 'if you can't beat 'em join 'em' option is virtually non-existent, intergroup conflict and political violence are much more likely to occur . Throughout this book social identity will be referred to in an attempt to demonstrate that this theory can shed light on the way we think, not only about the causes of conflicts, which often lead to political violence, but also about issues concerned with coping processes, moral development and most importantly ways in which to overcome intergroup conflict.

Before launching into more detailed considerations, it is necessary to take two important decisions concerning the subject of this book. These involve the questions of how to define what is meant by 'children' and what is meant by 'political violence'.

Defining Childhood

What is a child? This, one might assume, is the easier of the two definitions to make. However, while most (though not all) people would probably agree that childhood begins at birth, reaching agreement about the time at which childhood ends is much more difficult. As noted above childhood is itself a relatively modern concept. In the past children moved from a sort of limbo status to adulthood very quickly – perhaps as young as age 7 or 8. Since then, particularly with the 'discovery' of adolescence, the age at which children are thought to become adults has increased, but has also become increasingly unclear.

Part of the problem is that the age at which children cease to be regarded as children varies according to the context. For example, in certain societies that age at which a young person may be eligible for military service may be younger than the age at which he/she may vote or even legally consume alcohol. Often it is left to politicians and/or the legal profession to arrive at these definitions. This is especially true in societies where political violence exists. In such societies defining the age at which childhood ends in certain spheres can have important political ramifications. No politician wants to be accused of imprisoning children or worse killing children. The solution therefore is often to invent some other name for older children or even to redefine the limits of childhood itself. For example, In South Africa (Liddell et al., 1993), childhood has been generally defined as spanning the period from birth to 10 years old. However, between 10 years and 18 years, the term 'youth' has been commonly used. In Palestine on the other hand, during the Israeli occupation, presumably because of the active role played there by children in the Intifada, 'the Israel military's definition of the legal criminal age has been remarkably fluid. In 1987, it was 16; by 1988, 14; more recently it has been 12' (Usher, 1991, p. 15).

In the absence of any clear theoretical rational in this area, I will define childhood, for the purposes of this book, as broadly as possible as the period from birth to the late teens. This is roughly comparable to the UN Convention on the Rights of the Child which defines a child to mean 'every human being below the age of eighteen years . . .' (Article 1); the same UN Convention suggests that states should try to ensure that military service does not begin before the age of fifteen years (Article 38).

Defining Political Violence

Defining political violence is equally difficult. The starting point is quite clear however. Political violence, as noted earlier, is a form of intergroup activity and thus must be distinguished from interpersonal violence. Political violence is violence which is perpetrated by one set or group of people on another set or group of people who were often strangers to each other before the violence occurred. Again this is an important point that will be returned to in later chapters. For the moment it is important to note simply that this means that this book will not deal with violence towards children of an interpersonal nature, for example child abuse, where the abuser is often a family member.

Does political violence then simply mean war, and if it does, why not use the term war instead of the longer and more cumbersome term political violence? One reason is that the term war often implies a conflict between two nation states. However, Van den Berghe (1990) claims that around two-thirds of all the people killed by states in the period 1945–87 were the state's own citizens. Another reason is that, according to some, there is a vast difference between the impact conventional warfare can have on children and the impact of less conventional violent conflicts. For example, Gibson (1989, p. 660) argues that the conditions in settings of political conflict, 'characterized by chronic strife, high personal involvement and political, social and economic oppression', are so unique that the impact they have on children can not be compared with conventional warfare. The argument therefore is that if we only studied the impact of war on children we would be not be getting a complete picture.

In my view, however, this is too subtle a distinction to make, given the present state of our knowledge. Instead I prefer to recognize simply that 'there are gradations of the horrible' as Garbarino et al. (1991b) have pointed out. Indeed, they suggest that one criterion for assessing the barbarism with which a political conflict is being fought is the condition of the children touched by the war.

Again, no doubt, there is a legal definition of war. However, at any one time in recent history children all over the world have been suffering in what may not have been defined legally as war – Lebanon, South Africa and Northern Ireland immediately spring to mind. There have, however, been countless others which have not made the headlines, and therefore do not so readily spring to mind, but which have also touched the lives of thousands of children world-wide. For the purposes of this book, therefore, the term political violence will be used to include everything from conventional warfare to other small-scale acts of political violence, as long as they can be viewed as 'acts of destruction that impact on power relations in society' (Hoffmann and McKendrick, 1990, p. 14). This definition of political violence however begs a further question. What may be seen in one society as an act of destruction or indeed what may be seen by one group in a particular society as an act of destruction may be seen by others as 'normal behaviour'.

In other words, what constitutes 'political violence' is always a social construction (Hoffmann and McKendrick, 1990, p. 3). Therefore, while there will be no debate about the violent nature of such acts as shelling or street rioting, such things as detention without trial for example or the use of force to suppress a particular form of religious observance could, in the eyes of some, be more debatable.

In an attempt to overcome this problem, therefore, for the purposes of this book, political violence will be defined loosely to include all those acts of an intergroup nature which are seen by those on both sides, or on one side, to constitute violent behaviour carried out in order to influence power relations between the two sets of participants.

Why Psychological Effects?

Undoubtedly, political violence has the potential to impact on children in many different ways. It could be argued that the major impact of political violence on children is an economic one. This economic impact quickly reaches children in these societies by various routes. Trade and industry soon suffer and as a result fathers and mothers become unemployed, and so there is less money for family essentials such as food and fuel. Economic problems soon spread to other areas of society and soon there is less money available for government-sponsored services such as health and education which are crucial to the development of children.

In situations such as this governments often move expenditure from essential services to the armed forces. What is worse, this appears to be more likely to happen in the poorer countries of the world. One claim is that while military expenditure has increased two-and-a-half times since 1960 world-wide, the increase in the developing countries has been seven-fold. As an example Dodge (1991) cites military spending in Africa which he claims increased from $8.5 billion in 1970 to over $15 billion in 1987. This is compared with an allocation for health of around $3.8 billion.

What is more, these effects have a long-lasting impact upon a country's economy. For example, Smith and Zaidi (1993) report the results of a random sample survey of children under 5 years old in Iraq following the Gulf War while UN sanctions were still in place. They found that almost one-quarter of the children showed evidence of stunted growth – an underestimate they suggest due to survivor bias. Nor is this a new phenomenon. Three-and-a-half years after the end of World War II there were estimated to be more than 20 million children in Europe in a declining state of health; the majority of these were children whose 'families have never recovered from the shocks and losses inflicted on them by persecution or war' (McArdle, 1949, p. 297).

Why then confine this book to psychological effects? While not wishing to ignore political and economic effects these will not be the main focus of this book. The statistics reflecting this side of political violence are relatively freely available from international agencies such as the UN and others. Instead the present text will focus more on the social and psychological impact of political violence on children – an area where concrete evidence is much more difficult to come by.

In addition, the present text will concentrate mainly on the quantitative as opposed to the qualitative evidence. There have been several excellent qualitative or impressionistic books written, dealing with children and political violence (for example Coles, 1986; Garbarino et al., 1991; Rosenblatt, 1983). Such work, at its best, can provide an eloquent testimony to the suffering of children in various parts of the world such as the Middle East, South Africa, or Cambodia. However, not everyone is totally convinced by such non-quantitative evidence – especially, it might be argued, government agencies. There is a need therefore to complement the penetrating insights offered by existing texts, such as those noted above, with more empirical data. That is what this book will aim to do.

Restricting this text to such data will, however, have a knock-on effect where the scope of this book is concerned. This is because, for the most part, 'hard' data such as these concerning children and political violence are available only from more western settings, in particular, South Africa, Israel, the Lebanon and Northern Ireland. Much less empirical work has been carried out in, for example, Latin America or the rest of Africa, which is a major weakness in the existing literature and therefore in this book. In addition restricting this book to more empirical work means that the evidence will have to be evaluated keeping the problems faced by researchers in this area always firmly in mind.

Research Problems

However one defines political violence and indeed however one defines children, obtaining data about children in such contexts is not a straightforward task but one which raises serious research problems. Some of these problems are common to much of research with children while others are virtually unique to this particular topic. To be able to evaluate the existing research it is necessary, therefore, first to have some understanding of both these types of research problems.

All social scientists are faced with difficult methodological problems. Further, all social scientists who work with children are faced with special problems. To take one obvious example, not all children are literate and therefore cannot be expected to complete psychologists' favourite research tool – questionnaires. Researchers in the area of political violence have to deal with everyday problems such as these, and for those working in the Third World this can be a major problem. In addition researchers who work with children (in any setting) face special ethical problems. Because of this the American Psychological Association has issued ethical guide-lines for researchers who work with children, covering such areas as the child's right to refuse to take part in research, and the need for informed consent of both child and parents (or parental substitutes).

However, all researchers in this area, no matter whether they are interested in the impact of political violence on stress, or moral development or educational achievement for example, share some particular problems not common to workers in other areas. Before considering the results of research in later chapters, therefore, where research problems more specific to each particular area will be discussed, it is important to understand what these problems are. In this way readers will be in a better position to evaluate research on children and political violence and indeed better equipped to carry out such research should they wish to do so.

Quantitative vs. Qualitative

The first decision facing a researcher is often whether to adopt a qualitative or a quantitative approach. Both have their advantages, and the advocates of each often hold strong feelings about their chosen technique. The problem is that those who see at first hand the suffering of children may feel that reducing these events to cold statistics cannot possibly convey what such children may have experienced.

Some researchers are of the opinion that qualitative material simply does a better job of explaining the problems faced by those who live in areas dogged by community strife. They feel obliged to avoid what they see as the cold, clinical approach of the statistical or quantitative treatment of real children's lives (Garbarino et al., 1991a). For example, Bryce (1986, p. 15) notes of her interviews with women in the Lebanon that although her material will later be transformed into statistical evidence

> there may be more truth in the power and eloquence of these women than in the best designed and highly generalizable survey

> or experiment. They are describing the human condition – their condition and that of their children – in a desperate situation which has been created and maintained by man himself. (Bryce, 1986, p. 151)

Incidentally, this tension between these two approaches is not new. Cyril Burt (Burt and Simmins, 1942, p. 72) commenting on research in England during World War II noted that problems arose in the interpretation of the existing research because 'practical workers feel a deep distrust of the statistics so dear to the academic psychologist':

> This often means that the 'practical workers' are quite ready to assure the 'academic psychologist' that he has underestimated the number of sufferers (or it may be overestimated them, for the practical workers are not agreed amongst themselves) while at the same time they decline to say what number they themselves have observed, or indeed whether their conclusions are based on anything but personal impressions.

Fortunately, today more researchers appear to be happy with both methodologies, realizing that they should not be seen as contradictory, but rather as complementary. Therefore, as more researchers use quantitative techniques (e.g. content analysis) to examine qualitative data, and as approaches such as discourse analysis (Potter and Wetherell, 1987) become more common, the distinction between these two approaches will hopefully blur.

Research Design

For those who adopt a quantitative approach, designing research in areas to be carried out where political violence is widespread presents numerous practical difficulties. To begin with, there are the obvious problems such as the impracticability of carrying out research of a truly experimental nature. The two most favoured approaches are therefore either straightforward surveys or quasi-experimental designs.

Surveys are necessary in order to establish the degree to

which political violence has impacted on children in a particular society. They are however, not straightforward exercises in the sort of conditions that exist in societies embroiled in war or civil strife. An example of the kinds of problems that can be encountered has been provided by Bodman (1941) who carried out a survey in the English city of Bristol at a time when air raids were common. He describes how on one occasion the address he had been given proved to be a heap of rubble while at other times he had to contend with problems raised by evacuation, convalescence, and the absence of both parents on war work, all of which he noted 'necessitated many extra visits and a good deal of correspondence'. Because of problems such as these, very few surveys have been conducted in areas of political violence that are based on truly random samples.

Often researchers wish to compare children who have been exposed to particular acts of political violence (for example, rioting, shelling, police raids, etc.) with those who have not been so exposed. Or failing this, to compare those who have suffered frequent exposure with those who have only infrequently experienced the particular phenomenon. However, to comply with the technical requirements of experimental research children would have to be randomly assigned to the two groups. The 'experimental' group would then have to be exposed to some form of political violence and the 'control' group sheltered from it. This of course is ethically unthinkable. What researchers do instead is to wait for such 'experiments' to occur naturally. This compromise is known as a quasi-experimental design.

However, such quasi-experimental research design raises another important technical question. Imagine that rioting breaks out in a particular city and either during this or soon after a researcher compares the children in the riot-torn city with those from a comparable city which did not experience rioting. Any differences that are found are then attributed to the impact of the rioting on the children.

This, however, involves making one major assumption, which is that the children from the two cities were exactly the same before the rioting took place. This assumption has to be made, because what is missing from such a design is any form of measurement of the children before the rioting. This absence of before-and-after measurements in the area of political violence can thus present a serious obstacle to interpreting results from studies which adopt quasi-experimental designs. In particular, sorting out the roles of cause and effect with any certainty becomes almost impossible in the absence of longitudinal data.

While the ethical and technical issues outlined above that impinge on research design are relatively obvious, there are other less obvious ethical issues. Again these are problems that are common to all research conducted with children. Where research involves children and political violence, however, certain ethical issues assume a special significance. Of these perhaps the most important and at the same time the most difficult to deal with is the need to avoid harming the child psychologically. The APA guidelines indicate that even if a researcher simply suspects that psychological harm might arise from a particular procedure then the researcher is obliged either to abandon the research or to find other means of obtaining the information. For a researcher in a society where community violence is rife this can lead to some difficult decisions. Does this mean that children should not be questioned, for example, about atrocities that they have witnessed? Will the act of reliving such an experience be psychologically harmful or helpful?

Obviously a child who has witnessed such events knows that something is wrong in his or her society. But it is entirely possible that a child in another town some distance away may not know about the same incident. This in itself may be a question of interest to a researcher. Are children in other parts of the country in which the atrocities happened living in fear that the same thing will happen in their town, or are they living in blissful ignorance. An easy research problem? No – because as Jahoda (1963, p. 153) observed:

> Even in the course of the actual investigation, as an unintended consequence of merely trying to answer questions of a kind with which they were not normally faced, some children had a flash of insight; things suddenly fell into place, and they reached a

> new level of understanding . . . this can be brought about so casually and incidentally . . .

Therefore the researcher, who finds himself or herself in such a position, will have to decide if direct questioning of children may mean that the research procedure will actually make children aware of a possible threat to their lives, of which they would otherwise have been totally unaware. For researchers in this field, therefore, choosing a research design is nearly always going to be a matter of compromising between scientific and technical requirements, and the much more pressing ethical demands of the real world.

Data Collection

The actual way that researchers obtain information from children varies with the degree of normality obtaining in the particular society. Questionnaires and interviews are probably still among the most frequently-used techniques. However there may be circumstances when data-gathering techniques have to be tailored to a particular situation. For example, in certain societies, at certain times, children may be reluctant to talk face-to-face with an adult about their problems. Under these circumstances children may feel happier, for example, writing essays. This is a technique that has been used successfully with children in Ireland and the Middle East (Hosin and Cairns, 1984) and in Uganda and the Sudan (Dodge, 1990). Or a child may feel safer dealing with apparently neutral cartoon figures or drawings – a technique that Punamaki (1988) has used in Palestine.

Ethical issues, such as those noted earlier, can mean that researchers may have to adapt their data-gathering techniques to avoid, for example, sensitizing children to the negative aspects of their society, of which they may be happily ignorant, or about which it may be difficult to talk. In these circumstances it is necessary to ensure that the research methods used are politically possible and not hurtful without being useful (Yule, 1988).

For example, Cairns (1980) wanted to learn at what age

children in Northern Ireland used first names as cues to identifying a person's religious group membership. The problem was that simply questioning children about this in a straightforward way could easily have meant that the research interview would actually be an instruction session in sectarianism for the child involved. To overcome this problem Cairns instead presented the children with a randomized list of typical Catholic and Protestant first names as part of a memory test. A measure of category clustering was then applied to the lists of names as recalled by the children to see if there was any tendency to group together the Catholic and Protestant names. In this way the information required was obtained without the true nature of the test necessarily becoming apparent to the children taking part.

Observing children in their natural settings can be a rich source of data. Unfortunately such research is time consuming and therefore expensive to mount and so is the exception rather than the rule. Liddell (1994) provides a good example of this type of approach. Her study involved observing, at 30-second intervals, the everyday patterns of play and social participation of five-year-old children from four different communities in South Africa. This provided 1440 observations – a total of 12 hours.

Sometimes researchers turn to adults as sources of information about children – for example, parents and teachers may seem like an attractive alternative source of information which can avoid some of the ethical pitfalls of working directly with children. Unfortunately there would also appear to be a problem with this strategy. This was a problem first reported by Despert in 1942 in a study of pre-school children in the US at the time of America's entry into World War II. What she reported was that there was a tendency on the part of parents to minimize children's reactions. Since then similar reports have been noted on the part not just of parents but also of teachers and other carers (Sack et al., 1986).

This tendency on the part of adults to deny the suffering of children can distort results in more than one way. Problems can arise even if children themselves are to be interviewed or asked to complete a questionnaire. This happens because in most, if not all societies, researchers need the permission of adults before they can approach children directly. However, adults, for example head teachers, will often deny vehemently that any of their children could possibly be suffering in any way, and therefore will refuse to allow the children in their care to participate in research on the grounds that they are saving the researcher from wasting his/her time. Unfortunately investigators often fail to mention these problems in their published reports despite the fact that they may well distort results by influencing the samples that are available.

This adult resistance is well documented in a study by McFarlane et al. (1987) that investigated the impact of a bush fire on children in Australia. What McFarlane found was that response rates among the parents in the 'experimental' group – that is the parents of the children caught up in the fire – were markedly lower than those from a comparable control group. This, McFarlane noted, was a concrete example of the 'resistances experienced in setting up this project and maintaining adequate return rates', which was interpreted as an indication of denial on the part of the parents whose children were involved in the fire. Undoubtedly this is a problem that other researchers also face, but, as McFarlane notes, very few studies actually report refusal rates. Nor is the problem just confined to asking stress-related questions. Tolley (1973), researching children's views about war and peace, had over 30 schools refuse to participate in his study. More recently Pryor (1992), looking at attitudes towards the Gulf War, had at least 20 schools refuse to participate because the school personnel felt a need 'to protect students from further stress'.

Another source of data about children is official statistics and/or official pronouncements. For example, statistical studies of the numbers of children referred to psychiatrists or admitted to psychiatric hospitals can be of use to those who wish to know about the amount of stress suffered by children as a result of political violence. Again, however, this source of information almost certainly underestimates children's psychological problems because it does not include children suffering psychological stress who have not been referred for specialist treatment. As the claim is often made that children exposed to political violence do not suffer 'serious' nervous disorder, but rather tend to suffer 'mild and probably temporary nervous disturbance' (Burt, 1942) and are therefore not likely to see a psychiatrist, this is an important consideration.

Another problem with both clinical and referral, and admission, data is that they do not usually provide basic information on the background characteristics of the samples under study. This makes it impossible for researchers to disentangle the effect of political violence from that of other sources of stress – poverty for example.

As a rule these official sources become less and less reliable the more intense the political violence. Psychiatric services are seen as a luxury in many peaceful societies; in societies embroiled in political violence, therefore, they are often among the first to disappear. For example, in war-time it is not unusual for psychiatric hospitals to be turned into military hospitals thus distorting the statistics on civilian psychiatric casualties. Indeed, general medical services themselves may be rudimentary in times of civil strife, often only geared to physical casualties, again limiting the information available from clinical sources.

Also government statistics in societies where there is political violence must be treated with some caution. For example, what is one to make of the following from Dr. R. Percy Smith's official presidential address to the Section of Psychiatry of the (British) Royal Society of Medicine on 31 October 1916 – a time when Britain was two years into the most horrific of wars?

> It would appear to have been calculated by our enemies that the effect of raids by airships would produce a widespread terror in this country and that the sight and rumours of burning towns, destroyed dockyards, ruined homes and killed or injured civilians, would lead to clamours for submission and peace. It may be said, however, that although in many instances the effects on individuals have been very serious, the total effect on the population has been very slight. (p. 10)

Is this a dispassionate professional observation, or is it coloured by patriotic wishful thinking – does it matter that earlier in his speech Smith (1916) had referred to the air raids as 'attempts at terrorizing the people of this and other countries by various means of frightfulness'?

Obviously, for propaganda reasons, governments are not always anxious to draw attention to the stresses and strains that their civilian population may be facing and so may prefer to turn a statistical blind eye to such problems. Sometimes it would appear that children in particular are simply forgotten about in the collation of official statistics. For example, finding out how many children may have died in a particular society as a result of political violence may not be a straightforward exercise simply because the official statistics do not record the age of those who died. This certainly was a problem encountered in two widely differing societies – Northern Ireland and Zimbabwe – where researchers report that to obtain such information they had to resort to examining newspaper records (Cairns, 1987; Reynolds, 1990).

In the absence of official statistics researchers in the area of stress and coping often make use of clinical data. These are an important source of information usually consisting of reports from psychiatrists and psychologists who are treating the child casualties as they develop. However, there are numerous problems in generalizing from data on clinical cases. The most important problem is that the samples are usually only small fractions of the numbers of children caught up in political violence. So, while such studies are of great clinical value, they produce only a limited picture of the psychological sequelae of violent events among children in the community as a whole, and are not a substitute for accurate referral data, or for properly conducted surveys.

The Neutrality Question

Perhaps the most taxing question facing researchers who work in parts of the world where political violence is endemic revolves around the whole question of scientific neutrality. The problem almost certainly has its roots in the early professional education of child psychologists where they are taught that their discipline is a scientific enterprise, because it adopts the scientific method defined as:

> an attitude or value about the pursuit of knowledge that dictates that investigators must be objective and must allow their data to decide the merits of their theorizing. (Schaffer, 1989, p. 15)

However, working in societies where political violence is impacting on children can and does lead researchers to question this value-free scientific stance. For example, Garbarino et al. (1991a) note that keeping faith with the children of the war zones that they wrote about in their book *No Place To Be A Child* meant writing 'a very political' book. This they also note made 'some people uncomfortable'. They don't say who these people are, but one can guess that they include the authors themselves as well as their professional colleagues.

What such critics of this approach may not realize, is that while in our western psychological tradition direct involvement in political matters may be frowned upon, in societies engaged in political struggle, refusing to take a political stand as a professional may be considered immoral. This is because what the advocates of the value-free approach often fail to understand is that findings can be used 'both to nourish and to destroy human well-being' (Punamaki, 1988, p. 8). A good example of such a society is South Africa – a society where it is difficult to sit on the fence as a scientific neutral and where researchers have therefore had to face up to both sides of this coin (Swartz and Levett, 1989).

One danger of this is that both sides may avoid doing research with children if they suspect the results will not support their particular ideology. For example, the South African government, according to Liddell and Kvalsvig (1990), has been known to stop research of which it did not approve. This could be done by government departments refusing to provide the mandatory permits for research in certain areas. Or governments may suppress government-sponsored reports, once the research has been completed.

On the other hand, researchers in South Africa have also pointed to the fact that it has often been necessary to obtain permission from community leaders before research is undertaken. This process, according to Dawes et al. (1989), is important to establish trust between researcher and researched;

a process 'highly necessary in the emotionally-charged and suspicious climate at the time'. However, more than the simple establishment of trust may be involved in these preliminary interviews. In at least one case, the researchers and the interview team 'had to make clear their personal opposition to what had occurred in the area and to apartheid' (Dawes et al., 1989, p. 19). Without this declaration, they note, access to the area would not have been possible. Despite this Dawes et al. (1989) claim that they, and researchers like them, can still treat the data they obtained objectively, while at the same time maintaining a moral stand against apartheid.

Personal Problems Facing Researchers

A major result of these technical and moral problems is that carrying out research in the midst of political violence can often be a stressful experience for the researchers involved. This stress comes from two main sources. First there is the fact that the investigator may be placing himself or herself in actual physical danger. Most researchers are reluctant to write about this for various reasons and when they do, often play down the dangers involved.

> It was frightening to ally ourselves with the children of war. It sometimes meant putting ourselves in harm's way . . . At various times while researching and writing this book we were under surveillance by at least one country's intelligence service, were detained or questioned by soldiers and police. (Garbarino et al., 1991a, p. xxii)

Stress may also be involved because researchers know that they may also be placing the participants in their research in danger. This is not such a problem when the participants are adults who may well operate a 'Code of Silence' where particular community activities are concerned. However, where the participants are children this presents a special problem. Children may be innocent of the importance of the details that they are willing to reveal, perhaps about the night-time activities of big brother or daddy. For this reason many researchers working with children in conditions such as this will solve this problem by studiously avoiding questioning children about such obviously 'delicate' issues (McAuley and Kremer, 1990).

The problem of how researchers should behave in areas where political violence is on-going, of how to be sensitive to local issues, and the problem of how to deal with political pressures both from official and unofficial sources raises another question. This is, who is best placed to conduct research in such localities – local investigators or outsiders? One argument is that local researchers can be too close to the problem and they are thus 'intimidated by the appreciation of the complexity of the situation viewed from a vantage point, or perhaps disadvantage point of local knowledge' (Heskin, 1980a, p. 8). On the other hand, some have argued that outsiders, often stereotyped as academic tourists who make quick visits to the hotspots of the world currently in fashion, are handicapped by their lack of in-depth knowledge of the local culture. Once again this is a question which should not necessarily be seen in all or nothing terms. Both sides have certain advantages. What is needed in future is for visiting academics to make contact with local researchers, and for both to join forces in a combined effort.

Summary

Despite the fact that throughout history children have been exposed to political violence, until recently the topic has attracted virtually no attention. One explanation may be that children in the past were not seen as full members of society and/or that in the past political violence tended to involve civilians rather less than it does today. Another possible reason is that during periods of upheaval in society civilians' mental health becomes even less important than it is during periods of normality. Or governments may even wish to discourage evidence of civilian psychological suffering for propaganda reasons.

Whatever the reasons for the absence of such work in the past some research is now beginning to emerge. The growth however has been slow and the development patchy. Part of the problem is that researchers are thin on the ground particularly in societies where political violence is prevalent – mainly in the Third World. Also, there may be a feeling, particularly in the US, that much is already known about the impact of violence, at least criminal and domestic violence, on children.

This raises the question, why study specifically the impact of political violence on children? Research in this area is important because political violence affects the lives of so many children throughout the world. Also it has been suggested that political violence may have a greater impact on children compared with other forms of violence. Also research is needed which will shed light on how political violence may be brought to an end. Finally, it has been argued that the impact of political violence is of academic interest because, given its intergroup nature, it is so fundamentally different from interpersonal violence.

Before looking at this and other problems in more detail a major problem is how to define two key concepts, children and political violence. This is difficult given that both are in effect social constructions. To accommodate this, a broad definition of childhood as lasting from birth to late teens was adopted. Political violence was similarly simply defined as acts of an intergroup nature seen by both sides or one to constitute violent behaviour.

It could be argued that political violence is likely to have its most important impact on children in economic terms. Despite this, a book looking at the socio-psychological impact of political violence is needed, because information in this sphere is much harder to access, and because the potential for psychological impact is at least as great.

To assess this potential psychological impact it is necessary to have empirical as opposed to anecdotal evidence. For this reason this book concentrates on this kind of evidence. However, in order to evaluate such research, some knowledge of the research problems involved is necessary, in particular the important issues concerned with research design, and the way in which data are gathered.

Armed with this background knowledge we pass on to do two things. The first is to consider the existing research concerned with children and political violence in some detail. The first three chapters therefore examine the topics of stress and coping (chapter 2), the impact of political violence on daily life (chapter 3), and children's involvement in politics in the widest sense (chapter 4). In the second part of the book we stand back a little from these issues, first by reviewing the existing work, which is devoted to the search for peace (chapter 5), and by providing a critical overview of the whole area (chapter 6), focusing on what needs to be done, not just to understand better the impact of political violence on children, but to bring that violence to an end.

Overall therefore it is my hope that this book will make the existing research on children and political violence available, for the first time, to a wider audience. In this way the book will provide an introduction to this important topic and in turn act as a stimulant to further research. The aim however is not simply to provide an uncritical review of the literature. Rather the intention is to highlight strengths and weaknesses in existing knowledge, and to draw attention to methodological problems in the general area, and the possible ways in which these can be overcome with a view to strengthening future work on this most vital of topics.

2 Stress and Coping

It has now almost become an accepted part of social science folklore that war leads to a reduction in mental illness. Evidence for this dates back to at least the early days of World War I when, for example, in 1916, the Report of the Asylums and Mental Deficiency Committee of the London County Council, noted that 'for the first time since the Council has been the responsible authority decreases are recorded both in the number of patients under reception orders . . . and in the total number of lunatics'. The Second Annual Report of the General Board for Scotland, in the same year, also reported, that for the first time since the institution of the General Board of Commissioners in 1857 there was 'an absolute decrease in the number of all classes of the insane in Scotland' (Smith, 1916 p. 17). As Dr William Graham pointed out in the Annual Report of the Belfast District Lunatic Asylum for 1915, 'the interesting and at first sight paradoxical fact is that this diminution takes place at a time when we are involved in the greatest war in the history of the world'. Nevertheless, he added, 'the fact is indisputable . . . insanity . . . has lessened during the period of the War'.

Nearly a century later can we still speak with the same degree of certainty on this subject? In particular, can we generalize from these data to say that political violence has no impact on the psychological well-being of children?

The Resilience Debate

At first research appeared to provide a positive answer to this question – certainly research carried out during World War II, again in England, despite the initial fears of adults, even experts. As Vernon, a psychologist, noted in the early years of that war:

> All observers seem to agree that raids have even less effect upon children than adults. One might have supposed that they would be more susceptible to the operation of a 'fear instinct' which is stimulated by loud noises. Though sometimes frightened by the sirens or explosions when they wake up, those that I and others have observed go to sleep again remarkably easily. (Vernon, 1941, p. 471)

According to some war-time observers, for many older children the sights and sounds of air raids were seen as thrilling events (Crosby, 1986).

More objective evidence however indicated that, at the very least, a minority of children were affected by the air-raids. For example, a survey by Dudson (1941) reported that out of some 8,000 children approximately 4 per cent showed 'signs of strain'. This report is of particular value because it was a survey of the general school population and was made at a time when 'severe raids were occurring fairly often'. On the other hand, it is perhaps worth noting that this evidence was based on teachers' reports and not on direct contact with the children.

Since then research from different parts of the world has tended to confirm the general principle – that when children are exposed to political violence the expectation is that all involved will not suffer serious psychological consequences – although rates may be raised. Studies based on surveys of children in Northern Ireland (Cairns and Wilson, 1993), for example, have estimated that around 10 per cent of children may be 'possible cases' (according to the teacher-based Rutter scale). This compares with rates of around 6 per cent in societies not plagued by political violence – for example 6.8 per cent in

England (Rutter et al., 1975), 5 per cent for Norway (Vikan, 1985) and 6 per cent in New Zealand (McGhee et al., 1985). Evidence from South Africa (Liddell et al., 1993) suggests that even when children are exposed to the most severe stressors, still only about 50 per cent suffer psychologically, while in a study conducted in Israel during the Yom Kippur War (Milgram and Milgram, 1976) 75 per cent of the children's war-time anxiety scores were higher than their earlier peacetime scores.

The most vivid illustration of this phenomenon in the literature is provided by Bodman (1941) again from war-time England. His report is of particular value because he himself was on the scene almost immediately after the event. The incident he describes happened at nine o'clock at night during the early years of World War II in an English city – Bristol – where, in one raid, the children's hospital suffered a direct hit. Bodman (1941, p. 486) relates how he went immediately to the hospital, which that night contained 54 child-patients ranging in age from 2 months to 12 years and found soldiers

> crunching through a litter of broken glass, fallen plaster, and blown-in black-out material, picking children out of cots and beds and, tucking them under their arms, running down the steps and dumping them pell-mell into the lorry. The hospital was in darkness, and the only light came from the fires raging in the city below. A heavy barrage was in progress and heavy high-explosive bombs continued to fall quite close to the hospital. Most of the children were transferred by lorry to my hospital; a few babies were carried in the arms of the soldiers the quarter of a mile, while spent fragments of 'flak' were buzzing down freely.

As Bodman says, 'here then was a really traumatic incident'. Indeed he noted that he himself still felt a little frightened when he recalled it. However, what surprised him was that only 61 per cent of the children showed signs of stress, which for the majority lasted two to three weeks.

At the other extreme Allodi (1989) in a study of refugee families (using the Rutter Scale) produced results which suggested that there were no differences between a group of children whose parents had been tortured, compared with children whose families were simply refugees. Similarly Ziv and Israel (1973) compared children who had been subject to shelling and those who had not (in Israel) and found low levels of anxiety in both groups.

Part of the problem is how to interpret studies such as these. Is absence of symptoms in children such as these a sign of health or illness, of resilience or of traumatization? What about children who have 'become so accustomed to mutilated corpses that they show no reaction at all' (Ronstrom, 1989)? Is this a 'necessary defence mechanism', as Ronstrom suggests, or is this 'lack or scarcity of feelings' actually 'the most severe problem that arises in children exposed to war' (Punamaki, 1987).

Generally findings such as those outlined above have tended to be interpreted positively. As a result, the emphasis in recent writings has swung from worrying about the suffering of a minority of children, as a result of political violence, to curiosity about the resilience of the majority. Punamaki (1987, p. 20) has however, been particularly strident in her rejection of the resilience concept. According to her, studies which claim to show that children do not suffer unduly from the stresses and traumas of war, are open to severe criticism. In particular, she has gone as far as to suggest that social pressures are in part responsible for the results, or at the very least, that the findings may in part be due to inadequate research methods. Similarly Palme (1991) has complained about the 'massive denial' of children's suffering which leads even 'well-educated and well-informed people' to question 'whether war-affected children are traumatized or otherwise psychologically disturbed'.

More reasonably, Dawes et al. (1989) have suggested that the time has now come to 'correct the sometimes hysterical emphasis' on resilience. They argue that the pendulum has swung too far, so that now resilience 'has become as 'fashionable' as the earlier 'damage thesis'. Dawes and his colleagues do not, however, appear to be challenging the general idea that not all children necessarily suffer psychologically as a result of political violence. Rather they appear simply to be suggesting that there is now a real danger that research will tend to 'underestimate the very real instances of psychological distress that occur in contexts of violence' (Dawes et al., 1989).

Therefore, before going on to discuss the burgeoning research which is investigating how the majority of children may be coping successfully with the stress of living in a society where political violence is prevalent, it is necessary to examine first the ways in which children, even if in most circumstances a minority of children, actually suffer.

How Children Suffer: Acute Symptoms

The general research picture is that, depending of course on the nature of the particular precipitating event, only a small proportion of children exposed to political violence require specialist treatment. Such children, however, tend to show a wide variey of symptoms.

One of the first clinical accounts of such a child victim may be that given by Smith (1916, p. 19) who described:

> a girl aged 14 years, who had just arrived at puberty. There had been much sexual talk at a convent school she was at, about the invasion of Belgium and reports of rape and other horrors. She became excited, had the delusion that Germans were coming to attack her, was in great terror of everyone, mistook identities . . . was noisy and screaming, and had to be put under care.

A more detailed clinical picture has been painted by Fraser (1974), a child psychiatrist working in Northern Ireland some 60 years later – a time when street rioting was prevalent in Belfast. According to Fraser the typical child victim of this period was one who had been exposed to a particular violent incident that, at the time, had led to such things as a fainting fit, an asthma attack or sleep disturbance. Further these problems tended to continue after the precipitating event and often to become worse with the passage of time, not better. Indeed, the original phobic anxiety attack often generalized to other stimuli.

Both these accounts in general terms have since been reinforced by reports from other parts of the world. For example, Chiementi et al. (1989) reported a study involving over 1,000 children in the Lebanon where the most frequently noted symptoms included shouting and screaming, crying, hyperactivity, and psychosomatic symptoms.

More recently various researchers, for example Dawes et al. (1989) in South Africa and Kinzie et al. (1986) working with Cambodian refugees, have begun to suggest that children damaged in this way display a general set of symptoms which approximate the DSM III category of post-traumatic stress disorder (PTSD). This syndrome consists of:

> depression, psychic numbing, feelings of helplessness, anxiety, fear, instability agitation, low self-esteem, paranoia, confusion, inflexibility and suicidal feelings . . . the child may also experience sleep disturbances, hyper-vigilance, loss of concentration, loss of memory and psychosomatic disorders. (Thomas, 1990, p. 447)

In particular, there is the recurring suggestion, first made by John (1941), that such things as fear of the dark and nightmares may become worse some time after the actual stressful event.

Despite the seriousness of these individual symptoms, what is remarkable is that most studies agree that there is very little evidence that the majority of children exposed to political violence suffer *serious* pathological conditions. Rather the general conclusion is similar to that reported by Malmquist (1986) based on a study of children who had actually witnessed a parent's (non-political) murder. What Malmquist concluded was first that all children fitted the minimal criteria for PTSD but at the same time there was also a 'good deal of resilience' and that despite signs of anxiety, children 'did not collapse into psychotic states'.

Understanding Resilience

Why do more children not suffer more serious psychological effects when exposed to political violence? The most obvious place to look for a clue to the fact that different children react to political violence in different ways is to examine the different types of event that constitute political violence. For example, one suggestion has been that the more personally children are victimized the greater the risk of developing serious symptoms (Arroyo and Eth, 1985). One way of examining this would be to categorize the events that constitute political violence into those which, for example, are an immediate threat to life, those which contain the possibility of a future threat to life and those which are not life-threatening.

The large body of research conducted on the evacuation of children from English cities during World War II clearly indicated the importance of the presence of parents or permanent carers. This could lead us to subdivide the above categories into events such as those which lead to separation from parents or carers and those which do not, either on a permanent or a temporary basis.

This is a line of reasoning which I do not propose to follow, however. To begin with there is just not enough clear evidence available which fits even the small number of headings noted above to make such an exercise worthwhile. One explanation for this is of course that often studies which examine children exposed to political violence are dealing with children who have been exposed to a series of incidents, not simply to one unique event. Further, even if a researcher thinks that a particular study is dealing with reactions to a specific incident, unless a life history is available for each child, there is no guarantee that this is actually so.

Most important of all, it would appear that this approach would be unlikely to provide any incisive answers because as Ayalon (1983) has noted from his work in Israel, one of the most remarkable findings is that despite exposure to the same event some child victims emerge with specific syndromes while others appear to remain totally unscathed. A concrete example of this is provided by Milgram and Milgram (1976) who measured the degree to which children had been exposed to a particular stressor – having a family member killed or injured during the Yom Kippur War – and found no relationship between measured anxiety and the military involvement of the child's family.

Evidence to back up the Milgrams' conclusion that it is erroneous to assume that objectively equivalent stress situations elicit the same subjective reactions in children has been lurking in the literature for some time. For example, Bodman (1941), investigating the children caught up in the bombing of the children's hospital described earlier, provides a report of one boy (Robert, aged 11 years) who thought that the whole episode was thrilling and even wrote to the Prime Minister, Mr Churchill, to tell him so. Bodman was able to trace this boy at a later date and report that he had been transferred to another hospital in another town which was also bombed. Two months later he was in yet another hospital when the windows were again blown in by a near miss. Despite all this Bodman reports that 'beyond being rather excited, he was not upset'. Perhaps even more remarkably Milgram and Milgram (1976), noted that some of the children they studied before the outbreak of war and then after war had actually begun reported a lower war-time anxiety level in comparison to their earlier peacetime level.

Resilience and Personal Factors

To begin with researchers tended to explain the variability of children's responses to the stress of political violence by turning to the role of such things as the child's age, gender and personality as well as the child's immediate environment, in particular the family.

Age: Few studies have made a serious attempt to investigate the differing impact of political violence at different developmental levels. One reason is no doubt because many of these studies are based on relatively small samples or confined to one or two age levels only. Given these restrictions generalizations are difficult to make. There have, however, been some attempts to make educated guesses on this subject. For example, Dunsdon (1941), based on her sample of schoolchildren in war-time England, suggested that stress was at its lowest in the 2–5 years age group. It was among those children aged 5–7 years that psychological symptoms predominated, while as children got older (11–14 years) psychosomatic illnesses became more common. Fraser (1974) also suggested three age bands which he believed were related to the child's capacity to understand what was going on in Northern Ireland at that time – mainly street rioting. Below 8 years he suggested that children did not fully understand the danger and, therefore, were minimally affected. Adolescent and older youths did understand what was going on but were able to cope basically by resorting either to flight or action. The worst affected group in Fraser's opinion therefore were children from about 8 years to puberty.

Bodman's (1941) observations of children at different ages exposed to the trauma of the bombing of the children's hospital so vividly recalled earlier – however – appear to contradict the view that younger children are immune to stress in conditions of political violence. In particular, he notes that the children under the age of one year were most at risk of death from infection, which he concluded was evidence of lowered resistance related to their stressful experience. His paper describes child victims from as young as 10 months to as old as 12 years all of whom suffered as a result of their terrible ordeal and therefore suggests that at no age can it safely be said that children are immune from stress related to political violence.

And this is the conclusion that research which has looked at children traumatized for reasons other than political violence has tended to come to. Children at different ages may respond to stress in different ways, and different stressors may have a different impact at different ages. However, vulnerability to stress does not seem to increase or decrease markedly at any specific age (Rutter, 1983).

Lyons (1987) has reviewed post-traumatic stress disorder in children, and reached the same general conclusion – which is that there is no age at which individuals are immune to the effects of traumatic events. What he does suggest is that there is a tendency for different patterns of symptoms to be associated with different age groups. Thus infants suffering trauma are likely to show, according to Lyons, such symptoms as irritability, sleep problems, diarrhoea and separation anxiety, while pre-schoolers are likely to show these symptoms plus the problem of acting these out in play. School-age children are more likely to show what are thought of as typical PTSD symptoms, for example nightmares, and/or re-enactment. During adolescence the symptom pattern is more likely to be one either of withdrawal or aggressive acting out.

One assumption in the literature, at times unstated, is that children and young people always suffer *more* from the stress of war and political violence than do adults. Even this idea has recently been challenged by Klingman et al. (1993, p. 79). According to their evidence, obtained in Israel during the Gulf War, 'adults were the most fearful, followed by the elderly, and only then by children. Young adults and adolescents were perceived as being least fearful'.

Sex: While no clear picture emerges from the age literature the literature on gender in relation to stress and political violence is, if anything, even more confusing. This is surprising because the general literature on childhood (Rutter, 1983) appears to agree that, at least up to the age of puberty, boys are more likely to be at risk when exposed to a range of stressors. According to Punamaki (1989) this has also been the general pattern in studies which have looked specifically at the impact of political violence. At least one study, however, (Dawes et al., 1989) has reported a more complicated pattern which involved the interaction of gender and age. This arose because boys had a higher frequency of symptomatic behaviour than girls in the youngest age group, while by middle childhood the two were very similar. By adolescence, however, proportionately more girls than boys had PTSD type symptoms.

Both authors speculated as to why these particular patterns might have emerged. Interestingly, both agree that in a society caught up in political violence adults may be less sympathetic towards male children. Punamaki (1989) suggests that this may in turn cause parents to give boys less support than they give girls or indeed to respond negatively to their boys' distress. Dawes et al. (1989) on the other hand, suggest two possible explanations for the fact that older boys appear to suffer less. The first possibility is that the data are distorted due to the reluctance of boys, or of their parents, to report symptoms (suffering being seen as unmanly). In other words boys are really suffering but no one wants to admit this. The second possibility is that in most societies males, including young males, are able to take a more active part in the on-going conflict and that it is this active role which helps to reduce male vulnerability to stress associated with political violence (the role of boys as combatants is discussed more fully in chapter 4).

Dawes's suggestion that there are no sex differences in middle childhood, however, find no support in the study by Milgram and Milgram (1976) which, it is worth noting, is one of the better designed studies in this whole area. What makes this study special is that it includes a measure of anxiety obtained from the same 85 urban Israeli children, aged 10 – 11 years, about four months both before they were exposed to political violence, as well as a second measurement obtained during the event (the Yom Kippur War in 1973). What this study found was, that before the war, anxiety levels measured using a pencil and paper test were very similar to those obtained from a North American sample. Also, as in the North American sample, means were higher for girls compared with boys. During the war anxiety levels rose for all the Israeli children but this rise was greater for boys than for girls, with the result that the level for boys now exceeded that for girls – a reverse of the peacetime finding. The results of this study are particularly interesting because more recently Schwarzwald (1993) has reported that, among a sample of fifth graders in Israel during the Gulf War, those exposed to Scud missile attacks showed the usual pattern. That is, girls' symptom levels were higher than those of boys. Among children of the same age in areas not exposed to such attacks however, boys reported more symptoms than girls.

Personality: Although little research was conducted on civilians during World War I, an early suggestion was that 'the war had a particularly disturbing effect on those who were on the verge of breaking down or had had previous attacks of mental disorder' (Smith, 1916). Research with children during World War II appeared to confirm this. For example, a young English psychiatrist (Bowlby, 1940) noted in the early days of 1939, that where evacuation was concerned it was, contrary to expectation, the children who felt happiest at home who settled best in foster homes. In contrast children who felt unhappy and insecure at home found it most difficult to leave. Despert (1942, p. 78), summarizing a series of World War II studies on children felt able to conclude therefore that:

> . . . in every case where anxiety in relation to the war was reported or observed, the child had previously presented an anxiety problem, the reverse does not hold . . . (that is every child with anxiety problems before the war did not become more anxious).

Punamaki (1987) reviewing later work has come to much the same conclusion. In particular, she suggests that, broadly speaking, children can be categorized into two types. The first is the passive, withdrawn and introverted child. This is the child who, she concludes, is the most vulnerable and is likely to suffer emotionally as a result of exposure to political violence. At the other extreme is the active, extroverted child who is likely to resort to aggressive behaviour as a response to political violence.

However, much of this 'evidence' is basically speculation. There is relatively little hard evidence on this whole subject. This lack of evidence, it should be noted, applies to the relationship between stress in general and children's personality characteristics (Rutter, 1983). Part of the problem is the absence of studies in which a measure of the child's premorbid personality has been obtained – that is a measure *before* exposure to a particular stressor.

As noted above the study by the Milgrams is an exception to this rule. It is of interest therefore that the Milgrams found, in their sample of Israeli children, a negative relationship between peacetime and war-time anxiety levels. That is, there was a tendency for those with low peacetime anxiety scores to have high war-time anxiety scores and vice versa. Of special interest is the interpretation that they placed on this finding. Their suggestion was that the peacetime scores may have mainly represented a personality factor – *trait* anxiety, while the war-time scores more probably reflected *state* anxiety or anxiety felt in response to a particular stressor. If we accept this interpretation then what the negative relationship between these two measures could mean is that it was the most temperamentally anxious children who responded to the war with the least anxiety. Milgram and Milgram (1976) suggest that this may have happened because these anxiety-prone children had become accustomed to high anxiety levels in peacetime and therefore 'reacted with less additional anxiety to war'.

Unfortunately no attempt has yet been made to replicate these results. If they could be replicated they would represent a major step towards overturning what has become a truism in the literature, that when children are exposed to political violence it is the nervous child who is most likely to become more nervous.

Resilience and the Social Environment

An early hint that the child's basic temperament might not be the sole or even the most satisfactory way of explaining resilience to political violence appeared in German literature during World War I. Here it was reported (Noggerath, 1917 cited in Wittkower and Spillane, 1940) that 'during air-raids well-balanced children were indifferent, and anxiety and excitement were observed only in families where the parents were excited'. Similar observations were made twenty years later in war-time England leading the authors of 'The Cambridge Evacuation Survey' to suggest that the concept of the 'nervous child' should be broadened to include the 'nervous family'.

These conclusions were based on the observation (Crichton-Miller, 1941) that while children stood up to the bombing remarkably well, what they did not resist was 'the contagion of panic and hysteria on the part of their elders'. Clinical observations made in Northern Ireland by Fraser (1974) likewise suggested that the fears expressed by his child patients reflected largely what had been expressed at home by their parents. And it is not just overtly fearful parents who are likely to be a liability according to Ronstrom (1989). Parents can also transmit fear to their children 'through hidden and mixed messages', for example, the tendency to be overprotective, or to hold anxious discussions from which children are excluded.

The family and social support: What has interested researchers is the possibility that it is not just the presence of unstable parents that can lead to problems but that the obverse is true. That is that stable parents, even if not physically present, can be a crucial protective factor. This conclusion was based on observations again carried out in war-time England among child evacuees. This work indicated that contrary to expectations it was children from secure homes who settled best when evacuated from the cities to foster homes in the country. Further, while Bodman (1944) reported that children showed great adaptability to air raids he also noted that 'the strain of separation from parents by evacuation was generally greater and the effects more profound'. Since then researchers have noted that it is not just the separation from parents per se which is stressful, but also that separation increases the vulnerability of children to the various stressors of political violence (Protacio-Marcelino, 1989).

Over the ensuing years children in many different societies have been subject to evacuation and separation from their families. Ressler et al. (1988) have documented these upheavals in remarkable detail. In two chapters, in particular – 'Children in Emergencies' and 'Separation, Trauma, and Intervention' – they provide an excellent review of the literature concerned with the psychological impact of evacuation, concluding that when children and their families are separated during wars and/or refugee movements, the psychological risk for children is increased.

In general, therefore, those who have written about children and political violence appear have moved closer to the conclusion reached by Freud and Burlingham in 1943 when they announced with great certainty that:

> war acquires comparatively little significance for children so long as it only threatens their lives, disturbs their material comfort, or cuts their food rations. It becomes enormously

> significant the moment it breaks up family life and uproots the first emotional attachments of the child within the family group. (Cited by Ressler et al., 1988, p. 149)

Despite the fact that this statement has virtually become part of the accepted folklore surrounding the whole topic of children and political violence, not everyone is willing to accept Freud and Burlingham's basic premise.

> It has been claimed that a young child does not suffer emotionally from war experiences at all if the parents and especially the mother is able to maintain a stable relationship and if the secure structure of family life is not shaken. This statement is utterly unrealistic because war, by its very nature, disturbs and breaks up family life. It is often precisely the demands which war makes on families that produce disturbing effects on a child's psyche. (Punamaki, 1987, p. 27)

The problem is, which of these equally dogmatic statements to accept? The difficulty is that most of the evidence comes from clinical observations rather than psychometrically-based investigations. Generally, these have been accepted in a largely uncritical way. Even the English World War II evacuation studies may not be as methodologically perfect as the secondary literature often suggests.

These evacuation studies probably suffer from two major flaws. The first is that, even when the evacuated children were randomly selected for study, they may still have been a partially-selected group. This is because there is reason to believe that to begin with not all English city children who should have been evacuated were evacuated. This raises the possibility that those evacuated were already selected to exclude a proportion of those children with psychological problems.

A second problem is that the children who were most upset by the evacuation were those who were the first to go back home – often before research could get under way. These children therefore excluded themselves from the sample of those studied (Valentine, 1941). Also none of these early studies was designed specifically to examine the role of the family in providing social support during times of political violence. However, more recently several studies have attempted to do just this.

In Israel, Meijer (1985) compared two cohorts of boys, one born in the year of the Six Day War (N = 57) and the other born two years later (N = 63). The children were seen as babies and later in first grade. Data were available from both mothers and teachers and from clinic files. Overall there were significant differences between the 'war' children and the controls.

For example, the war children were significantly delayed in terms of speech and toilet training and in learning to walk. Later, at school, differences were found on a Clinical Child Psychiatric Questionnaire with the war children more likely to have bowel problems, to be rated by teachers as more socially withdrawn, irritable, less considerate and more resentful, and by their mothers as less calm and less likely to be eating well. The authors suggest that these differences were possibly due to lack of support for the mothers plus the 'high state of tension' of the mothers at the time of the war. On the other hand, they do acknowledge that they had no specific data on the mothers at this time to back up this assumption and therefore it is possible that other factors could have played a role in the differences between the two sets of children.

Data relating to mothers themselves were obtained in a study by Bryce et al. (1989) carried out in Beirut. This study set out to investigate the relationship between the psychological functioning of both mothers and children (152 aged 5 years to 7 years) in Beirut in 1984/5 and mothers' experiences at that time. Mothers completed the Beck Depression Inventory and also responded to a 19-item check-list for child behaviour. One of the study's interesting findings was that mothers' level of depressive symptomatology was the 'most important predictor of reports of child morbidity'. This, in turn, was no doubt related to that fact that mothers who responded emotionally to events in Beirut at this time were more likely to also respond emotionally to their children. However, the authors point out that these finding have to be treated with caution because the reports of the child's illness might have been biased by the mother's ability to remember symptoms, her experience in recognizing childhood problems, and social desirability (this could have been exacerbated by the fact that interviewers were local people). Another study in the Lebanon (Chimienti, Nasr and Khalifeh, 1989) has provided information which the authors claim goes some way to overcoming some of these problems. This involved children (1,039 aged 3–9 years) from three cities where political violence had been particularly rife. The children in this study were divided into those who had experienced personal trauma such as death of a family member or forced displacement and those who had not experienced such a trauma. Each mother completed a questionnaire concerned with their children's emotional and social behaviours and also answered questions about their own reactions to the political violence. Their results indicated that 'trauma-yes children were about 1.7 times more likely, compared with trauma-no children, to exhibit symptoms and behavioural problems'. Chimienti et al. (1989) examined the possibility that a mother's own stress reactions influenced her perception of her child's reactions. What their results indicated was that mothers tended to report similar general reactions for themselves and their children, but where more specific behavioural reactions were concerned, mothers' reports of their children's reactions were relatively independent.

At about the same time Dawes, Tredoux and Feinstein (1989) were conducting a similar study designed to explore the impact of forced removal from a squatter community in South Africa on a non-random sample of 71 families who had at least one child aged between 2 and 18 years. Some three to four months after the evictions, data, based on interviews with the parents, were collected in order to estimate the incidence of PTSD in the adults and the incidence of emotional, conduct and physical disorders in the children. Again the interviewers were indigenous people. Results suggested that some 63 per cent of the women and 32 per cent of the men were suffering from PTSD. Around 9 per cent of the children were also thought to be suffering from PTSD while another 32 per cent were reported as suffering symptoms but not PTSD. In other words 59 per cent of the children were reported to be symptom free. The comparison of the relationship between maternal mental status and child symptoms (Dawes et al., 1989, p. 30) indicated that:

> children were as likely to develop a single symptom of stress whether their mothers showed serious stress reactions or not . . . [however] . . . children whose mothers were diagnosed as having PTSD were significantly more likely to have multiple symptoms of stress than were those whose mothers were not so diagnosed.

Unfortunately, there are several related problems with all of these studies. To begin with, as noted above, the study by Meijer (1985) was unable to produce any objective evidence that the mothers studied had indeed suffered from the effects of stress. This was not a problem with the studies by Bryce et al. (1989), Chimienti et al. (1989) and Dawes et al. (1989). The main problem with these studies is that they rely entirely on the mother to provide information both about herself and about her child.

One study which did obtain independent data from both child and mother was that carried out by Punamaki in 1982. This study involved children (8–14 years) and their mothers living in the West Bank and Gaza Strip. Mothers' symptoms were obtained using a screening test while children's psychological symptoms were assessed by the mothers (using a version of the Rutter). In addition the children evaluated themselves (using a version of the Children's Manifest Anxiety Scale and a fear scale). Several papers have reported on the results of this study. In the first (Punamaki, 1987) the results indicated that maternal depression was related to the mother's assessment of her child. Also children's fears were related to the mother's ways of coping and her religiousness. Child anxiety, however, was related only to the sex of the child. These results Punamaki (1987) noted confirmed earlier suspicions that 'a mother's mental health and behaviour are important in affecting her child's psychological well-being in a stress situation'.

In a second report Punamaki (1989) presented data from (apparently) the same 105 children from the Occupied Territories (referred to as the 'stress' group) plus 30 Palestinian children living 'within the 1948 borders of Israel' (considered to be a 'control' group). Initial comparisons of the stress and control groups indicated that the 'stress' groups had higher levels of psychological symptoms and anxiety but similar levels of fearfulness. The remainder of the analyses appear to have been carried out on the West Bank/Gaza children only. This involved comparing those whose mothers reported that the family had been exposed to many events related to political violence with children who had not been so exposed.

These analyses revealed, somewhat surprisingly, that there were no significant effects of family happiness on children's symptoms, fears or anxiety, nor was there any interaction between these factors and exposure to political violence. On the other hand, there was an indication that exposure to political violence increased children's anxiety levels but only if the mother displayed an external locus of control. Mothers' use of 'social-political activity' as a coping mode also appeared to be involved in decreasing her child's symptoms but in elevating her child's fears. Finally, children with many symptoms tended to be those who were exposed to many political violence incidents and whose mothers also had many symptoms. In the same way a mother's level of depression was related to her assessment of her child's symptoms, but not to the child's own assessment of his or her fears and anxiety.

The final report of this study was authored by Punamaki and Suleiman (1990). This report used data from 66 children in the stress group with equal numbers of boys and girls. This time the analyses placed more emphasis on the role of the coping modes of the children rather than the mothers. What is interesting is that these analyses indicate that the children's symptoms (as rated by the mother) were correlated positively with their own coping processes and the mother's symptoms. However the child self-assessed anxiety levels correlated positively only with the mother's internal locus of control concerning the Palestinian issue. Internal locus of control was in turn associated with exposure to higher levels of political violence. Also this study raised, for the first time, the possibility of a relationship between a mother's symptoms and the child's coping mode. In particular, it was suggested that the more mothers admitted to symptoms the more likely their children were to employ 'active and courageous' coping modes.

In her conclusion to the 1989 paper Punamaki noted that the results only 'conditionally' agreed with the observation that the way mothers respond to stress caused by political violence will be a factor in determining children's mental health. The limitation, she suggested, was that when political violence increased, only an internal locus of control on the part of the mother is able to act as a buffer for the child. Punamaki then went on to list three factors which, in her opinion limit the relationship between the role of mothers and children's mental health. First she noted that at high levels of political violence the mother's health was bound to be affected and thus it was unlikely that the mother could act as a buffer. Secondly, she suggested that the role of acting as a buffer in the face of enormous difficulties was itself likely to be a stressor for the mother. Finally, she noted that in this area it is difficult to determine cause and effect. In other words it is difficult to say if it is emotionally-upset parents who lead to emotionally-upset children or vice versa.

From a methodological point of view Punamaki's study illustrates the necessity of having evaluations of mother and child which are independent of each other. What her results confirm is that the relationship between stress on the part of mother and child is mainly found when the mother is the source of both evaluations – as in many of the studies noted above. However, in the Punamaki study the child's anxiety level, and the child's fears appear to be independent of the mother's symptoms, and coping style.

Punamaki's work, at the very least, illustrates that this is a much more complex area than had hitherto been suspected. It is badly in need of replication in another culture and with differing levels of political violence. What the outcome of such a replication might well demonstrate is that mothers can act as a buffer but only at moderate or low levels of political violence. When political violence reaches literally unbearable levels then it may be that there is little that mothers can do to provide psychological protection for their children. In such circumstances having children to protect may be an additional stressor for mothers.

This work also needs to be replicated with groups of children at different age levels. The child's age may also determine how effectively the mother may feel she can offer protection. For example, it may be easier for mothers to provide psychological protection to pre-school children but not to adolescent children, particularly adolescent boys who are more likely to become involved in the on-going political struggles as combatants (see chapter 4). Finally, an important question is can the experience of family life support provide long-term as well as short-term protection for the child exposed to political violence?

Other sources of social support: Future research, in particular research which involves school-aged children, needs to broaden the concept of social support and to focus less exclusively on mothers. This would bring the political violence research more into line with recent research on social support which has tended to define social support as a perception on the part of the child that he or she is cared for, esteemed, and valued by members of his or her social network (Cobb, 1976). Already there are some indications in the literature that mothers are not the only sources of support for children caught up in political violence. For example, some observers of the English evacuations noted that children suffered fewer problems if they were billeted with their siblings (John, 1941). Also it has been noted that family members other than parents, for example grandparents, can provide emotional security during times of political violence (Protacio-Marcelino, 1989).

Social support can however also come from sources not actually within the child's family. As Ressler et al. (1988) point out in their review of research on refugee children, during times of heightened threat the community can be an important source of support for children, with the community being widely defined as 'relatives, teachers and other familiar adults'. To this group should of course be added other familiar children.

Again the World War II literature carries hints about the importance of the role of this wider community. Pritchard and Rosenzweig (1942), for example, considering the problems of evacuation in England noted, somewhat enviously, that in Germany things had been done differently – and perhaps rather better. There, school classes were kept intact and were evacuated with their teachers plus the Hitler Youth leaders who had been their counsellors in the schools at home.

Others have similarly commented on the role of the wider community. For example, Ziv and Israel (1973) found low anxiety levels in Israeli kibbutzim children and suggested that this was due to the social support provided by 'the highly cohesive setting in which kibbutz children lived' plus the confidence which the children placed in the Israeli army. Other observers in Israel have suggested that the amount of previous experience a community has had with political violence and the general preparedness to meet 'unpleasant life events' is also related to the amount of support that the community in general can provide (Ayalon, 1983). Finally the social support network has been cast even wider by Protacio-Marcelino (1989) who has suggested that one buffer against stress in the Philippines has been 'the emotional support from human rights groups within and outside the country'.

Resilience and Appraisal

Recently, while still emphasizing the role of social support the literature has come to be dominated by the cognitive – phenomenological model of coping (Lazarus and Folkman, 1984). Cognitive-phenomenological theory suggests that two processes are involved in the relationship between stress and psychological adjustment – appraisal and coping. Initially, through appraisal, the individual evaluates the personal significance of the stressful situation. Then, in a manner which is contingent upon the outcome of appraisal, coping regulates the way in which the person thinks and behaves in relation to the stressful experience. This of course helps to explain why different individuals can appraise the same event differently or indeed different events similarly and in turn why different individuals may adopt different coping strategies.

According to the 'stress and coping' framework, the psychological outcome of a stressful experience depends on the way the stressor is evaluated (appraisal) and the strategy used to deal with it (coping). As Rutter (1983) has noted, although the appraisal process has rarely been considered in children it is highly likely that a child's primary cognitive appraisal of the positive or negative meaning of a particular life event will determine whether that event is experienced as stressful or not.

A major gap in this area concerns the child's sources of information about the on-going violence that enables appraisal to be carried out. One obvious source is the parents, particularly the mother. Bat-Zion and Levy-Shiff (1993) have produced evidence which suggests that young children may not engage in much cognitive appraisal because they rely almost totally on parental emotional cues to interpret threatening situations. However, so far no research has been undertaken to find out what mothers actually tell their children about political violence or indeed what messages, verbal or non-verbal, children get from their parents. It is therefore worth considering that this may be another important variable that will help explain the protective role of mothers discussed earlier.

Another possible source of information, which needs researching in today's age of mass communications, is the media. For example, Figley (1993) observed that during the Gulf War families of US service personnel experienced the biggest impact of the war as a result of watching television news 'even sacrificing other activities to do so' (p. 334). In Northern Ireland, where the violence has received extensive local media coverage, research has shown that not only adults but children are exposed to television news broadcasts and that for some children at least this is an important source of information on this subject (Cairns et al., 1980; Cairns, 1984; Cairns, 1990). This research has established that even children who have not been personally exposed to the violence, because they do not live in areas where violence has occurred, have acquired relatively detailed information about such things as what the 'confidential phone' is used for and what rubber bullets are. However this research has also claimed that exposure to television news broadcasts has not distorted children's ideas about the level of violence in their neighbourhood (Cairns, 1990).

Television coverage of the violence in Northern Ireland while it has been extensive has been remarkably restrained. This almost certainly accounts for the contrast between the conclusion reached in Northern Ireland and preliminary findings involving children in Kuwait following the Gulf War (Nader and Pynoos, 1993). In Kuwait many children were apparently exposed to horrific sights on television. As a result the research indicated that the single best predictor of the children's scores on a PTSD measure was 'witnessing mutilated bodies on television'. Television viewing, Nader and Pynoos (1993, p. 194) concluded, however, was not a primary cause of PTSD in children. Rather they suggest that 'in the absence of the ability to maintain a psychological distance 'seeing death, blood and mutilation on television . . . increased the severity of PTSD reactions'.

As yet few studies have deliberately set out to study children's cognitive appraisal of political violence and relate it to stress levels. There is, however, incidental evidence that such appraisal may be important. For example, in the early years of the air raids in England Harrison (1941) noted that it was not the most heavily-bombed civilians who suffered the worst forms of anxiety states. Instead, it was those who lived in areas that had narrowly escaped bombing that suffered most. This Harrison dubbed 'anticipation neurosis'. A concrete example of this phenomenon is attributed to Anna Freud (Pritchard and Rosenzweig, 1942). Her story concerned a boy aged 4 who was one of the few children in her children's home who had never actually been bombed, and yet appeared the most nervous of all her children. His playmate, a girl of the same age who had had a very narrow escape when a bomb blew off the roof of her house, was heard to advise her nervous friend, during an air raid, that he should pull the bedclothes over his head when the guns got noisy. More recently observers in both Northern Ireland (Fraser, 1974) and in South Africa (Liddell et al., 1993) have also suggested that it is not the event itself that may be critical in determining childrens' reactions to political violence, but rather the child's interpretation of the event.

This is an area that is badly in need of research. At the moment we know little except that, where children are concerned, 'objective and subjective danger may be weakly correlated at best' (Garbarino et al., 1991b). This is what emerged when Cairns (1984) carried out research in two low violence towns in Northern Ireland and two relatively high violence towns – the violence levels being objectively determined according to deaths per thousand of the population (Poole, 1983). In each of these same-sized towns children were asked to say if there had been 'much trouble' in their district in the last three years by responding on a scale from 'none' through 'some' to 'a lot'. As expected more children in the 'violent' towns thought 'some' or 'a lot' of violence had gone on in their town (46 per cent compared to 27 per cent). However, what this also means of course is that the majority of children in the 'violent' towns thought their towns were not violent while almost one third of the children in the non-violent town apparently thought violence had been taking place there.

Similarly, Schwarzwald et al. (1993) asked Israeli children, who lived in areas either attacked or not attacked by Iraqi missiles during the Gulf War, to complete a scale measuring levels of damage to property and injury to people in their region. The mean score felt the children who lived in the region *not* attacked was not zero as one might have expected. Incidentally, Schwarzwald et al. (1993) labelled this scale an 'objective' measure of stress!

These results are of interest for several reasons. To begin with they raise the possibility that either habituation or denial may be operating among these children, a point that will be returned to later. Secondly, they also suggest that children are not reliable sources of 'objective' information about violence levels in their neighbourhoods.

Therefore, where political violence is concerned, we appear to know less about the impact of subjective factors than we do about that of objective factors. We have limited evidence, for example, that such things as the child's proximity to the violence, the intensity of the event, the number of events the child has been exposed to and the length of time that the violence lasts can be important and positively correlated with stress levels (Milgram, 1993). What we know less about, however, are those variables that influence the symbolic and personal meaning of the event for the child, such as the child's religious or political orientation and the coping processes that the child is likely to adopt.

Religion: One factor that could influence the meaning of an event for both child and adult is religion (Park, Cohen and Herb, 1990). Indeed, these authors suggest that religion may influence both primary appraisal and the choice of coping option (secondary appraisal). This is an area which Roe (1993a) has explored in a South American context, examining the role of local churches and what are referred to as 'Base Christian Communities'. Yet to date researchers investigating the impact of political violence on children have almost totally ignored religion. The literature does contain tantalising allusions – but no hard evidence. For example, McWhirter (1983) has suggested that the Christian churches in Northern Ireland may have had a positive influence on children's coping in Northern Ireland. In Zimbabwe Reynolds (1990) has recorded the work of spirit healers who played a role in the healing of children caught up in the war there.

Of course as Roe (1993a) has noted, in settings of political violence while religion can assume an adaptive role it can also hinder positive development. For example, he suggests that while religious fatalism can provide short-term relief it can also impede efforts towards community development. Indeed 'extremist religious ideology can permit conflict and suffering to be interpreted . . . as a commitment to "the struggle"' (Roe, 1993a).

Given the importance of religion in many if not most of the regions of the world where political violence is rife and its positive and negative potential in the lives of children in these conflicts; this is an area that deserves closer attention.

Politics: In many parts of the world where political violence is found, politics and religion are so intertwined as to be virtually indistinguishable. Regardless of which is the principal ideological source either, or both, can be an important psychological resource during times of political violence. As noted above they may act to show the way in which events are appraised. In this respect politics and/or religion may play a role in the development of external attributions for political-violence experiences. Such attributions, it has been suggested (Joseph et al., 1991), are related to better psychological outcomes following stress-creating events than are internal attributions. Certainly observers at different times and in different contexts have noted that an ideological dimension 'emerges repeatedly in accounts of families under stress' (Garbarino et al., 1991b).

One problem where the role of ideology is concerned is that almost certainly it is confounded by other factors. For example, Vernon (1941) observed that giving children a task which involved taking responsibility for others reduced anxiety in war-time England. What may be really important therefore is not ideological commitment per se but the fact that children and young people who become involved in politics have an opportunity to play an active role in what is going on around them. This explanation would also fit in with the phenomenon of anticipation neurosis noted above, if one assumes that when actually under attack or in the thick of things, children are more likely to be active. Frequent reports of increased aggressive behaviour among children exposed to political violence may also be explained as a form of active coping (see chapter 4). Punamaki (1987) has however, questioned the coping role of activity suggesting that it only serves to delay the outbreak of symptoms at best.

Also it is likely that ideological commitment may in turn be related to group membership. This of course means that because of their ideological commitment children may belong to a group from which they receive social support. This is not to suggest that political commitment may not of itself play a role in helping children cope with the negative impact of political violence. For example, Ziv et al. (1974) interpreted a higher level of local patriotism among children exposed to shelling in Israel, as evidence of active coping. In Northern Ireland McWhirter (1990) has suggested that for some young people being an active protagonist has had a positive influence which enhances self-esteem. Evidence to back up this idea has come from a study (Punmaki, 1996) in which the role of ideological commitment (operationally defined as 'glorification of war', 'patriotic involvement' and 'defiant attitudes towards the enemy) in moderating psychological symptoms was examined among 385 Israeli 12 year olds. What this research suggests is that exposure to political hardships increased suffering but only among those children with weak ideological commitment. It is important to note, however, that this protective role for ideological commitment occurred mostly among those children who had been exposed to the lowest levels of political violence only. Similarly Punamaki (1988, p. 5) has pointed out that for many children perhaps caught up on the fringes of political violence, 'their personal happiness is dependent primarily on the collective well-being and political success'. This indicates a line of research that needs to be developed further. This is the role of social identity as a coping process in terms of Tajfel's Social Identity Theory (see chapter 1 for more details) which predicts that self-esteem is influenced by social identity as well as by personal identity and is a theme that will be returned to in chapter 6.

Resilience and Coping

To the casual observer it is not clear that active involvement in political violence can always be relied on to be an effective coping mechanism. The problem would appear to be that this form of active coping can lead, not to a reduction, but to an increase in personal hardships, for example, to imprisonment and increased harassment by security forces (Punamaki and Suleiman, 1990). Despite this it is important to note that ideologically based activity still remains a likely coping process. As Folkman and Lazarus (1988) have pointed out coping should not be thought of as being synonymous with mastery over the environment. Many sources of stress cannot be mastered. In these circumstances effective coping is 'that strategy which allows the person to tolerate, minimize, accept or ignore what cannot be mastered'.

Denial/distancing: It could be argued that at least a problem-focused coping strategy such as ideologically-based activity does not distort reality. The same cannot be said for the other coping mode which is most frequently mentioned in the literature on children and political violence – denial/distancing. Unfortunately, once again no studies have actually set out to measure this process in children exposed to political violence. However, over the years researchers have interpreted certain behaviours of children faced with political violence as evidence of the operation of denial. Gillespie (1944) noted that in wartime England it was not uncommon for children to refuse to talk to adults about a stressful incident while at the same time talking, for example, to their dolls. Yet another suggestion is that children who are apparently excited, perhaps laughing while in a stressful situation, are displaying a denial reaction (Fraser, 1974). Klingman et al. (1993) interpreted the fact that after the Gulf War Israeli children sent messages to US soldiers stationed in Israel which carried positive verbal messages written on drawings which depicted negative emotions, as indicating that 'deep feelings' may have 'been repressed or denied at the verbal level' (p. 89).

In the same vein Kinzie et al. (1986) have reported that the adolescent children they studied who survived concentration camp conditions in Cambodia were, as a result, 'private, subjective and characterized by denial and avoidance of thinking about their problems . . .'. McAuley and Kremer (1990) have suggested that sex differences may be involved. Their research took place in a community in Belfast where 85 per cent of householders (adults) interviewed reported that they had had their homes searched by the security forces, while some 50 per cent reported that they had received threats from security forces. In the same community children (aged 10–11 years) were asked to indicate if they had experienced particular aspects of the on-going political violence. Over 80 per cent had seen such things as hijacked vehicles burning, bomb scares, and soldiers searching for people. More serious events had been experienced by somewhat fewer children – people shooting guns (50 per cent girls; 66 per cent boys) and a bomb exploding (32 per cent girls; 43 per cent boys). What led McAuley and Kremer (1990); to speculate that girls 'may have been using a denial technique to counteract anxiety' was the fact that girls tended to report that they had seen fewer violence-related incidents and, that for girls only, the number of types of incidents seen was related to self-assessed anxiety.

Finally Rofe and Lewin (1982) have produced some tantalizing data as a result of their comparison of Israeli high school children living in a border town with those from a similar town in the centre of the country. What they found was that children living in the border town reported that they went to bed earlier, fell asleep earlier and had fewer elements of aggression and violence in their dreams. The reason for this Rofe and Lewin decided was that the children in the border town had developed repressive denial mechanisms in order to cope with the ongoing political violence that they had been exposed to since early childhood. Unlike most researchers in this area Rofe and Lewin (1982) were able to produce some evidence to back up this assertion because they had asked their children to complete a repression-sensitization scale. And what they found was that children from the border town scored significantly higher on this measure than did the children from the non-border town. In other words what they appear to have found was that children in the border town had developed a way of coping by avoiding thinking about potential danger.

Habituation: In 1943 Geddie and Hildreth (1944) carried out interviews with children aged 6–7 years in New York during which they asked questions such as 'have you heard about the war' or 'do you like to play war?' In the same year Rautman and Brower (1945) showed elementary school children in Sioux City ten TAT pictures and asked them to write stories about each picture. The stories were then scrutinized for mentions of the war.

As a result of their study Geddie and Hildreth (1944), who found for example that none of their young subjects failed to name Hitler as a war leader, concluded that 'these children had more current information about the war than the investigators assumed would be shown' (p. 97). In contrast Rautman and Brower (1945) concluded – having found that some 62 per cent of the children made no mention of the war, and only 6 per cent produced a story with a 'frank war theme' – that the children as a group 'did not seem to be unduly preoccupied with war or war activities' (p. 201). The way that these two apparently contradictory results should be interpreted, I would suggest, is that children in the US took the war for granted unless encouraged by a researcher to think directly about it.

McWhirter (1988) also reached a similar conclusion after reviewing a series of studies in Northern Ireland. She noted that the more ambiguous the research procedure adopted, the less likely children were to refer spontaneously to the on-going political violence. Based on this and other data McWhirter came to the conclusion therefore that for the children of Northern Ireland 'abnormality had become normality'.

This idea in turn encapsulates a weaker version of the denial/distancing hypothesis which is that children cope with political violence either because they place a deliberate emphasis on the normal things of life (Yule, 1988) or because they become so accustomed to political violence that political violence is perceived as normal (McWhirter, 1988). Both Yule and McWhirter had children in Northern Ireland in mind when they made these observations. Similar suggestions have, however, been made regarding children in South Africa. There, according to Liddell et al. (1993) whole communities which have suffered oppression have been socialized into 'the expectation of abuse' so that they interpret political violence as 'normal and unremarkable'.

One might imagine, therefore, that habituation is only likely to become an effective form of coping in a society where political violence has existed for some time as in South Africa or Northern Ireland. Such a suggestion fits in with the the immunization model which suggests that if people survive stressful events this leads them to be better prepared to meet the next stressful event (Breznitz, 1983).

There are, however, also some indications that children may habituate (that is, become accustomed) to political violence remarkably quickly. For example, Klingman et al. (1993) report that several studies of Israeli children found a significant decline in stress reactions from the first to the fourth week of the Gulf War. Relatively rapid habituation to political violence may not be a new phenomenon either. Some 80 years earlier Kimmins (1915) noted that when he asked children, who were living in London during World War I, to write about the war, very few mentioned the blackout of the street lighting. As he remarked 'it would appear that in the eighth month of the war the children had become so accustomed to the darkening of the streets that it ceased to be of interest to them' (p. 152). This evidence in turn may lend credence to Rachman's (1990) suggestion that habituation is based on decreasing uncertainty because people tend to, initially, expect higher levels of anxiety than they actually experience.

Long-Term Effects of Stress

The June 1992 edition of a British Psychological Society publication *The Psychologist* carried a letter, signed by 80 Yugoslavian psychologists, which contained a heartfelt plea for support for the children of Yugoslavia. The letter ended with the warning that if nothing was done these children might develop 'into substantially impoverished generations of emotionally unstable, intellectually incompetent, socially limited and intolerant individuals . . .'.

This is not a new concern. Rather it is a spectre that appears to haunt adults in virtually every society where children are exposed to political violence. Even when children appear to be relatively resistant to the immediate stress of war, what has worried adults, including psychologists, for some time, is that 'it may well be 15 or 20 years before any true estimate can be made of the psychological damage that has been done' (Pritchard and Rosenzweig, 1942). Nor has increasing knowledge about coping processes diminished this fear. Now the question being posed is – does coping entail a cumulative cost (Heskin, 1980b) and in particular what is the relationship between short-term coping and long-term aftereffects (Palme, 1991)? Is it correct as outlined in Breznitz's (1983) 'exhaustion model' that people may eventually run out of psychic energy if they find themselves having to cope with stress over a long period of time.

Put simply, one possibility is that staying apparently unaffected, without showing any emotions, will exact a psychological price which will only become evident when the coping processes are no longer needed. Another possibility is that having to cope with traumatic events in childhood will predispose individuals to disorders later in life *if* they are again exposed to stressful events (Rutter, 1983). In contrast, some observers have considered that surviving a stressful experience in childhood can have positive consequences later in life either because this allows particular coping mechanisms to develop or because it has some general toughening effect.

Holocaust Survivors

The largest source of information in this area to date has come from studies of Holocaust survivors. McArdle (1949) provides some interesting contemporary reactions to Jewish child survivors in the immediate post-war years. In particular, she was able to obtain information about such children who survived the concentration camps and were brought to the US for resettlement. Apparently the people involved in this work were initially apprehensive about what sort of task they were taking on. Their notes, written at the time, indicate that these children did not immediately slot back into a normal life style. On the contrary, the fears of their hosts were well founded, with some children initially behaving 'like animals at meal times' and many others distrustful and frightened. Jealousy and greed were also noted plus aggressiveness. What is more, these unpleasant behaviours apparently tended to increase when the children were placed in hostels. However, according to McArdle (1949, p. 247), after a short time 'suddenly an amazing relaxation took place' and in the long term the children were freed from their 'obnoxious traits and habits'.

Yet the horrifying ordeal that the children had been exposed to left a more permanent mark on some, according to McArdle (1949). Some wanted ceaselessly to repeat stories of horrific experiences such as shovelling ashes in the crematorium and cutting down hanged men from the gallows. Some children recounted these events without showing any signs of emotion, apparently thinking 'it obligatory to speak with an air of callousness about such things' (p. 242). Others could not bring themselves to mention such things without falling into 'fits of rage'. And among some child survivors 'there were some in whom melancholy brooding had spread deep roots and the habit of sorrow was ineradicable' (p. 259). Overall, therefore, according to McArdle (1949), it is futile to generalize about such children because their reactions varied enormously from apathy to rage although survivor guilt was a relatively common emotion. On the positive side observations made at the time suggested that self-reliance was a widespread characteristic.

By the 1960s work with survivors of all ages in different countries had begun to agree that a constellation of symptoms could be identified which became known as 'The Concentration Camp Syndrome' (Eitinger, 1980). The syndrome consisted of symptoms such as depression, anxiety, irritability and restlessness. These were often accompanied by guilt feelings, nightmares and general alienation. This research also suggested that the more severe the stressors to which the survivor had been exposed the more severe the symptoms evident in the CCS. Needless to say survivors also suffered from physical diseases and almost certainly for this reason psychosomatic complaints were common. While not all survivors suffered severe psychopathology occasional reports have painted a blacker picture. For example, Krupinski (1967) suggested that, among immigrants to Australia, those from Eastern Europe who had experienced Nazi concentration camps showed the highest incidence of schizophrenia.

As a result of this research Shanan (1988) concluded that 'for nearly half a century it has been clear that morbidity and mortality . . . among Jewish Holocaust survivors . . . far exceed rates in normal populations, even in non-Jewish survivor populations . . .'.

However, this research did not make clear how prevalent CCS was among survivors. This is because virtually all of the work had been based on contact with survivors who had sought help from mental health professionals. Therefore while the literature was often interpreted as implying that CCS was virtually universal among Holocaust survivors there was, to begin with, actually little or no evidence to back up this assertion.

This situation was remedied by the publication of Shanan's (1988) study which suggests that among survivors CCS was not a universal phenomenon. As part of an on-going longitudinal study Shanan was able to identify matched groups of Jews who had either survived a concentration camp or had lived in Israel during World War II. What was unusual about this sample in the context of Holocaust-survivor research was that it had been chosen so as to include 'normal' people, who were gainfully employed, physically and mentally healthy and aged around 46–65 years at the time of first contact. What was noteworthy about Shanan's results was that there were no significant differences in terms of personality or coping strategy between the survivor and the comparison groups. The only difference was in the realm of cognitive functioning. This indicated a lower intellectual performance on the part of survivors. Shanan (1988) concluded therefore that even under the most adverse conditions 'a *very* small minority of people' could adapt in a way which safeguarded their subsequent long-range personality development.

Some suggestions as to how survivors, including those of the Holocaust, might have coped will be considered in the next section. For the moment however, it is important to acknowledge, especially where the Holocaust survivors are concerned, that the issue of coping relates mainly to coping with the after-effects, as opposed to the actual experiences of concentration camps. This is important because the question of how people actually survived the concentration camps themselves is a contentious one. Some writers have argued that there is absolutely no evidence that surviving the concentration camps was 'due to anything more – or anything less – than luck and fortuitous circumstances' (Dwork, 1991, p. xxxiii). Dwork, in a strongly worded statement has rejected the idea that survivors employed some special survival strategy or enjoyed a 'special will to live' as 'not only arrant nonsense but a pernicious construct' (p. xxxiii). Dwork (1991) rejects these ideas because, according to her, the logical outcome of this argument is that those who died in the concentration camps are in some way to blame for their own deaths.

> It suggests failure or stupidity on the part of those murdered . . . the implication is that those who did not survive were undeter-

mined, weak-willed and irresolute; ... in a word inferior. (p. xxxiii)

Refugees

Of course, it is possible that the Holocaust may have been so atypical that the evidence noted above is of limited use in determining the long-term effects of 'normal' political violence. Since World War II countless thousands of children have become refugees as a result of more 'typical' acts of political violence. Ressler et al. (1988) provide an excellent review of research in this area. No studies, however, appear to have followed up survivors of this experience over a long period of time as has been done with Holocaust survivors. The medium-term follow-up research that is available, however, appears to be mildly optimistic about the long-term psychological consequences of this experience.

What is becoming clear therefore is that coping processes can be employed to ward off the medium-term as well as the short-term effects of trauma. Shanan (1988), for example, suggests that in his sample 'denial and isolation' may have played an important role. Also observations of child refugees suggest that social support may not only play a role in coping with on-going trauma (as noted earlier) but may also provide some sort of long-term protection. Basically the suggestion is that social support may act as a buffer to the long-term effects of trauma (Sack et al., 1986) thus facilitating what Ressler et al. (1988) refer to as children's 'recuperative potential'. For example Sack et al. (1986) followed up 170 Cambodian young people who were settled in the United States and found that some 67 per cent could be described as 'not mentally ill'. Among those who were considered ill the most common diagnosis was PTSD. In contrast Miller (1969) found only minimal evidence of PTSD in a sample of Guatemalan refugees. One possible explanation for the difference between the results of these two studies is that one group was now living in a culture very different from their native culture (the USA) while in the second study the children remained in a rather more similar culture with the prospect of one day returning to their home-land. Further, the latter children appear to be living in well-contained communities which had assimilated little of the host community life.

This latter effect has, for example, been documented by Kinzie et al. (1986) in a study with children who had escaped from concentration-camp-like conditions four years earlier in Cambodia. What their results showed was that these children were less likely to be diagnosed as suffering from PTSD if they were living with a family member or with a foster family. The role of social support in the aftercare of survivors had of course first been demonstrated with children who had survived the experience of the Nazi death camps. Here work, such as that carried out by Anna Freud in England, had shown that in the absence of family, well-run institutions could play a role in nourishing the 'high potential for recuperation of such children, even among those more emotionally unstable children who often developed severe neuroses only after their release from the camps' (Garmezy, 1983). In such institutions the role of social support arising from well-developed peer relationships also proved to be a valuable psychological asset (Freud and Dan, 1951).

Remarkably, there would also appear to be evidence that the impact of social support can outlast its origins. In other words that social support can provide a measure of stress inoculation to children which acts to help them avoid the long-term effects of trauma. Evidence for this comes from the research on refugee children reviewed by Ressler et al. (1988). What they suggest is that children who had experienced supportive family relationships prior to the loss of their parents and their flight from their homeland are better placed to recover psychologically in the long-term. In particular, they suggests that paradoxically remembering the happy family life that they had led before becoming refugees is both a source of sadness and also a source of psychological strength. This was a phenomenon also noted among Jewish-child survivors of the Holocaust (Dwork, 1991). Among these children 'who were old enough to remember, the memory alone of family life was a source of strength and solace' (p. 262). This means, that the age at which a child becomes separated from his or her family is important. Ressler et al. (1988) suggest that the loss of both parents before the age of 5 is, therefore, most likely to place a child at risk, if another satisfactory relationship with an adult does not develop.

Whether this optimism generated by the short- to medium-term studies of survivors will be justified in the long-term is questionable, according to the findings of Ettinger and Strom (1981). Their work first followed up a sample of Norwegian ex-concentration camp survivors over the period 1945–65. What they reported was higher mortality and psychiatric morbidity rates over these periods compared to the Norwegian population. However as Eitinger and Strom (1981) noted, these results left open the possibility that this was not a permanent phenomenon. If one assumes that the prisoners with the lowest resistance would be most likely to die first, then this raises the possibility that the phenomenon of raised mortality and morbidity rates would in time disappear. This hypothesis was, however, refuted when a further follow-up of those still alive during the 1965–75 period again revealed raised levels of mortality and morbidity rates.

More studies such as this have now been completed, for example studies of World War II combat veterans (Hierholzer et al., 1992), prisoners of war (Eberly and Engdahl, 1991), and resistance veterans (Hovens et al., 1992). These and other studies (see Wilson and Raphael, 1993 part III) are beginning to indicate that for some people the effects of stress can last a lifetime. However what is missing from this corpus of research to date, is lifetime follow-up studies of child survivors. It still remains a possibility that children's capacity to cope may provide them with better long-term protection as some claim it does in the short-term.

Bereaved Children

From an epidemiological point of view bereavement can be considered an ordinary life-experience (Horowitz, 1993). However from a clinical perspective 'the death of a loved one, especially a shocking or unexpected death, is well beyond the ordinary range of experience for that individual' (p. 55). Political violence, whatever form it takes, often leaves many fatherless (and to a lesser extent motherless) children in its wake.

Despite this there are very few studies in this area. Perhaps professionals have ethical problems in dealing with such children because they are basically afraid of further traumatizing them (Pynoos and Eth, 1985). Whatever the reason there is very little research and in particular there is very little information about children who have witnessed the violent death of a parent (Black et al., 1993) as children often must do in societies exposed to political violence.

Milgram (1982) has however provided a brief review of the small number of studies which have been carried out in Israel on children made fatherless as a result of war. This research suggests, perhaps not surprisingly, that children in Israel whose fathers died in war suffer from both behavioural and emotional problems. Further, what evidence there is suggests that these problems may continue for some years after the precipitating event. For example, a follow-up of two families ten years after a parent was killed as a result of terrorist activity in Israel indicated that the children, now young adults, despite initial short-term gains, showed signs of 'pervasive long-term symptomatology' (Dreman, 1989). These cases illustrated that adjustment could be influenced by situational factors such as further terrorist activity retriggering or exacerbating post-traumatic symptoms.

Unfortunately, virtually all of these studies, as Jensen and Shaw (1993) have pointed out, are inadequate because they lack a control group of children bereaved for reasons other than war. This makes it difficult to decide if the impact on children of father-loss as a result of political violence differs from the effects of bereavement under other circumstances. Therefore, while there may be no research to back it up, investigators tend to harbour the suspicion that bereavement due to political violence may be different from bereavement during peacetime conditions because 'in conditions of political violence the context and meaning of the loss may have a unique significance' (Jensen and Shaw, 1993, p. 701). For example, in certain circumstances the lost father may be regarded as a particular hero by the grieving child or there may be circumstances in which the local community and/or the nation is able to share the child's grief.

Summary

This chapter has examined evidence on the topic which has attracted most attention in relation to children and political violence – that of stress and coping. To the uninformed adult it must seem inevitable that every child who is exposed to political violence will suffer serious psychological consequences, serious enough that is to warrant specialist help. What the empirical evidence suggests is that such suffering is not inevitable even if children are exposed to exactly the same incident. The proportion who will suffer probably depends of course on, among other things, the exact form that the political violence has taken.

This conclusion is based on relatively sound evidence that has been accumulated over the last half century. The only weakness in this area, it could be argued, is that researchers have tended to rely too heavily on teacher and parental estimates of child stress levels, with not enough direct measures from children themselves.

The children who do suffer sufficiently to be considered clinically ill appear to experience a wide variety of variety of symptoms. Until recently these have not been thought to form a specific constellation but more recently the whole constellation tends to have been referred to as PTSD. Perhaps the most salient characteristic is that symptoms tend to become worse with time not better.

The realization that children show resilience even when exposed to political violence has led investigators to search for those factors which may be helping at least some children to escape the more severe forms of stress. Early candidates in this area included personal factors such as age, sex and personality. Surprisingly very few studies have examined these in any systematic way which makes it difficult to draw clear conclusions.

For example, no clear picture emerges where age is concerned so that even the idea that children suffer more than adults has recently been challenged. Similarly, unlike the general developmental literature the results concerning sex differences are contradictory. Even the accepted wisdom that anxious children are more vulnerable when exposed to political violence appears to receive little sound empirical support. In fact the best empirical work in this area so far by Milgram and Milgram (1976) suggests that the opposite may be true.

Another part of accepted wisdom in this field is that social support is the key to resilience. This may be provided, according to some sources, either by the mere presence of one or both parents (but especially the presence of the child's mother) or more specifically by the presence of a parent/mother who manages to remains calm in the face of political violence.

While this may be true, how important the role of the family will actually be is almost certainly related to the degree of political violence. Obviously families find it increasingly difficult to function as the level of political violence increases. Also it appears likely that the relationship between the child's level of functioning and that of his/her family will eventually be seen to be much more complex, involving not simply mother and child health levels but also the coping patterns adopted by both mother and child.

Overall, however, despite the importance of this question, much of what we known about this topic is based on anecdotal evidence or clinical insights. The empirical evidence, while it is growing, remains weak because of the absence of studies in which the child's psychological health is assessed independently of the mother's.

Additional sources of social support have attracted speculation, including the extended family, the child's peers and the wider community. Here the evidence is almost entirely anecdotal but provides many interesting ideas that warrant empirical investigation.

The cognitive-phenomenalogical model of coping may indicate a way forward in this area. While no research with children exposed to political violence appears to have consciously adopted this model it is possible to find empirical evidence that is generally supportive. For example, there is some weak evidence that the child's religious and political beliefs may influence the way in which political violence is appraised. What we appear to know almost nothing about is children's sources of information regarding political violence and how they evaluate these sources.

There is speculation that appraisal is likely to lead children to cope with the stress of political violence by employing denial and/or distancing. In contrast to this some investigators would argue that what has been labelled distancing/denial is in fact habituation. Both denial/distancing and habituation are difficult concepts to define operationally. It could be argued, however, that there is some weak empirical evidence to substantiate the habituation hypothesis.

A major problem with this whole area is the almost complete lack of studies in which children have been seen both before and after their exposure to political violence.

Finally, this chapter reviewed the long-term effects of exposure to political violence. Three hypotheses have been entertained as to how such exposure during childhood could influence later adult psychological health. For example, it has been suggested that coping may involve a cost that will be seen in later life, that coping may predispose one to later problems, or that on the other hand exposure to stress during childhood may have a toughening or steeling effect.

Evidence from Holocaust survivors probably provides the largest source of information on this subject. Here it appears that claims of universal difficulties in later life have possibly been exaggerated. In contrast, evidence from children who become refugees is mildly optimistic, at least in the medium term. Here the role of the child's pre-refugee family support is emerging as an important factor. Again, much of this is based on weak evidence. Unfortunately studies in this area often lack adequate (or any) control groups, while samples may be biased when they are obtained from clinical sources.

3 Everyday Life

As noted earlier, little is known about the more subtle effects of political violence on children; in particular little is known about its impact on their everyday lives. This chapter will therefore examine evidence that focuses on the home, the school and play. In addition we will consider how these factors combine to influence children's development in two important and related areas – those of aggression and moral development.

Before doing this, however, we will turn briefly to an area that has been virtually overlooked by researchers in this field. It has been claimed that while the direct effect of political violence is relatively easily seen and most easily dramatized it is often the 'prosaic and unobtrusive' influences that have the greatest effect (Titmus, 1950). We will therefore begin by asking whether political violence can have important indirect effects on children?

Indirect Effects

This is what Bryce et al. (1989) found in the Lebanon. Poor families were more likely to have direct experience of the violence and also were more likely to report that the violence had a negative impact on their lives. Similar evidence comes from another survey in the Lebanon (Armenian, 1989). This survey revealed that symptoms of psychological distress occurred more frequently among children from families that had suffered a major loss of income since the war began. It would therefore appear, as Garbarino et al. (1991b, p. 150) have put it, 'social class does not take a vacation in a war zone'. Either poor families are already on the brink, and political violence pushes them over it or wealthier families simply have the means to escape the worst ravages of political violence – or both. In other words, not only do the usual problems that children face not evaporate because of the onset of political violence, but it is likely that there is a cumulative effect with the negative consequences of political violence added to the effect of economic and social disadvantage.

Evidence to substantiate this observation has come from a study by Garbarino and Kostelny (1996) that involved interviews with 150 Palestinian mothers and their children caught up in the Intifada. What they were able to show was that while exposure to political violence was related to children's problems (as reported by mothers using the Achenbach Child Behavior Checklist), family negativity, which included such things as intra-family violence and maternal depression, had an even greater impact. As a result they concluded that, given the overall correlation between family dysfunction and lower socio-economic status observed in most societies, the children most vulnerable to the effects of political violence are likely to be those among the poorer sections of society. The important point, therefore, is that psychologists, social scientists and others interested in the impact of political violence on children should remember, that for many of these children it may not be psychological stress or impaired moral development that is their main problem. Instead as commentators in such diverse societies as the Philippines (Protacio-Marcellino, 1989) and South Africa (Liddell et al., 1993) have noted it is 'simpler' things such as inflation – leading to outrageous prices in the shops – and general poverty, which often have the biggest impact on children. As a result, as McCauley and Kremer (1990, p. 24) pointed out in their study of a community in Northern Ireland:

> while the conflict has played an important part in the lives of the people . . . at the same time the problems which are created

> by social and economic deprivation . . . have a more immediate and less avoidable impact on day to day existence.

Further, as the severity of political violence in any society increases and the infrastructure begins to crumble, this in turn can have a major influence on children's lives. For example damage done to institutions such as hospitals and schools may mean that children's physical health will be put at risk. Of course it is often difficult to disentangle the physical and mental elements that accompany the long and exhausting struggle that is required to survive in the midst of political violence. In the worst of situations children's lives may be affected by such things as lack of shelter, poor diet and lack of medical services which in turn may lead to increased susceptibility to simple diseases such as diarrhoea, respiratory and childhood infections, and to a general increase in the child-mortality rate (Armenian, 1989; Arroyo and Eth, 1985).

One of the best documented illustrations of the indirect threat to children posed by political violence comes from England in World War II (Titmus, 1950, p. 33). For young children in particular he notes,

> accidental death, in simple and unexpected dress, was never far away. The war with all its drabness, darkened rooms and stairways brought it perceptibly nearer. Mothers stumbled in the gloom; mistakes were made with food and drink; the sudden note of the air raid siren, summoning fear, or the shuddering whine of a bomb, brought flurried haste and anxiety.

Titmus backs this claim up with statistics which show, for example, that in 1940, the first year of heavy air raids in England, a sudden rise in the number of children burnt or scalded to death was apparent. Also, during the early years of World War II more children were suffocated in their beds. These statistics show that for the under fives the number of children who died in this way rose by 60 per cent in 1941 but declined after that. 'Suffocation of food' was another increased cause of death, this time among babies during the first years of the war, as was 'accidental swallowing of a foreign body'.

One of the more perplexing statistics to emerge from World War II in England was the fact that road accidents increased considerably – by 25 per cent in the first year of the war and 20 per cent in the second (Lewis, 1942). According to one report at the time, this increase could not be explained by obvious factors such as fewer police on traffic duty, or that lighting restrictions were in place, especially the latter, as most accidents actually occurred during the hours of daylight. Of particular interest is the fact that, according to Titmus (1950), the number of adult deaths from road accidents fell. While at the same time many more children were killed in this way. What is more, an apparently similar phenomenon has been reported in two other societies suffering from the effects of more recent political violence. In South Africa one of the major causes of death among South African teenagers is motor vehicle accidents (Malteno et al., 1986) while in Northern Ireland deaths from road accidents have exceeded those due to political violence in almost every year since the violence began. Also, in Northern Ireland there has been quite a close correlation between the two so that as deaths from political violence increase so do deaths from road accidents.

In the past psychological explanations for everyday phenomena were not so popular as they are today. It is all the more remarkable, therefore, that such an august body as the Royal Society for the Prevention of Accidents should, in 1940, suggest that 'mental stress' was a likely contributory factor leading to the increase in accidents in war-time Britain. Malateno (1986) commenting on the South African data speaks of a 'love of risk taking' while noting that it is also tempting to speculate that this phenomenon could be attributable to the externalization of aggression. Certainly this is a phenomenon that deserves further scrutiny.

Whatever else all of these statistics tell us, they emphasize the point that political violence does not take place in a vacuum (Bryce et al., 1989) and that the daily lives of children in areas of political violence are subject to many of the same crises found in more peaceful parts of the world.

Family

Given the importance of family life to children's development under normal circumstances the impact of political violence on the family is a much under-researched area. The literature does, however, contain some tantalizing, often contradictory, insights. Obviously much will depend on the level of political violence obtaining at the time, but where this reaches a peak then family life may disintegrate almost completely. In certain circumstances this may be because the family is directly threatened by the political regime in power at the time. For example, there is some evidence that the Pol Pot government may have made a deliberate attempt to break up families (Ressler et al., 1988). In other societies the same goal may be achieved indirectly because parents have been killed or incarcerated for political reasons (Protacio-Marcelino, 1989).

In extreme circumstances, therefore, as Garbarino et al., (1991b) have noted parents can be 'pushed beyond their stress-absorption capacity' and when that point is passed 'the development of young children deteriorates rapidly and markedly'. Even where the family remains intact the impact of political violence may throw the family into a state of crisis for economic reasons if no other (Bryce et al., 1986). In other situations, as noted in chapter 2, living with the stress of political violence, particularly when the stress is chronic rather than acute, may actually strengthen family bonds.

Almost certainly the common experience lies somewhere between these two extremes. Reports from several societies, for example, Cambodia (Sack et al. 1986), have suggested that despite deterioration in economic and living conditions the traditional role of the family can be maintained. But whether the family operates in exactly the same way that it would in non-violent societies is not clear. Instead, families almost certainly adapt to the changed circumstances and, like individuals, learn to cope. In these circumstances families still probably provide their children with the minimum environment for normal development.

Of course, in many societies, adult male members of the

family especially, get caught up in the political violence. This may lead to their death or imprisonment or simply their absence from home for long periods. Figley (1993) suggests that children from families which include a combatant, may suffer either from what he calls Secondary Traumatic Stress Disorder or from Tertiary Traumatic Stress Disorder. The former, it is claimed, is more common among older children and is an anxiety disorder produced by concern for a traumatized person. The latter is an anxiety disorder produced by concern for a secondary victim, for example the mother, and is more likely to be shown by younger family members.

Figley's (1993) ideas are relatively new, and originate from his involvement with families of US troops during the Gulf War. Despite this, the literature does contain some examples of the phenomenon he has attempted to label for the first time. For example, as will be discussed later in this chapter, father absences have long been associated with increased levels of juvenile delinquency during war-time. Also, the death of a father in combat or even his detention for involvement in politically-motivated violence, has been known to be associated with such things as behavioural disorders. For example, Dyregrov and Raundalen (1987, p. 117) report that following the October War of 1973 Israeli children in general coped well but that those who lost their father were more likely to have 'severe and persistent behavioural problems'.

Protacio-Marcelino (1989) gives a graphic account of families in the Philippines where children had to come to terms with sudden, involuntary and long-term separation from their fathers. This, she notes, not only led to emotional distress but 'severe disruption' of the whole family including perhaps moving house and/or neighbourhood. Also, not uncommon in situations of political violence are cases where members, often the male members, of families find themselves, for various reasons, on opposing sides. In these circumstances the impact on the family can of course be devastating and affects the family's role in providing succour to its younger members.

For these reasons in many societies where political violence is rife families are often headed by women, rather than men, and the responsibility for the family is likely to be borne by the mother alone. In such situations the mother may be the breadwinner as well as catering for the family's domestic needs while at the same time trying to act as an emotional buffer between her children and the stresses of the outside world. Sometimes neither parent is available to fill this role and older children take on the responsibility of looking after their younger siblings (Dyregrov and Raundalen, 1987). This, of course, not only affects the other children in the family, but undoubtedly has a constricting impact on the life experiences of the child who takes on the adult role.

Parenting Styles

Research workers in several different societies have commented on the fact that, even when the family remains relatively intact, the stress imposed both by economic circumstances and by the political violence can lead parents to feel overwhelmed by their responsibilities. One common solution to this situation appears to be to resort to a more authoritarian model of child rearing. This has been noted in work with torture victims in Chile (CODEPU, 1989). The existence of family violence has also been commented on in work from the Philippines (Acuna, 1988) and from South Africa (Dawes, 1992). The question of cause and effect is not however clear in all of these cases. It is not clear if this is a child-rearing style that is adopted in response to the stress of political violence or if it is a style which predated the onset of political violence. If the latter is true, it could be argued that authoritarian parenting styles should be seen as a cause of political violence rather than an effect.

However, some work which strengthens the possibility that political violence leads to authoritarian parenting and not vice versa comes from work in the Lebanon (Bryce et al., 1986) where mothers reported that they often resorted to physical violence with their children. More importantly, the authors were able to show that the more depressed mothers were the more likely they were to respond emotionally, by getting upset and/or hitting their children.

> Of course I've changed a lot during the war. I fight a lot and I get angry easily. You can't even bring a child up as you should, so how can you deal with a man? Now, if my child comes to me and asks me for water I feel like killing him and telling him to get off my back. I am not patient with them, so how can I be patient with my husband? . . . At times I wish I could lock myself in a room and not see anybody or do anything. I can't tolerate anyone, even my children. (Mother of 3, Beirut quoted in Bryce, 1986, p. 130)

Even where parents are not forced to resort to physical violence they may still feel the need to impose on their families 'a restrictive and punitive style of discipline' in an attempt to protect them from the dangers of the environment around them (Garbarino et al., 1991b). Clear evidence for the adoption for such a parental approach comes from a study carried out in Northern Ireland by Whyte (1983). Whyte asked 12 year-old children about such things as 'who decides what you can watch on TV' and 'do you normally do such things as wash your hair, or take a bath on your own, or switch off your own light at night'. The children came from three areas, one with no political violence – an inner city suburb of London, a second with limited political violence – a Protestant part of east Belfast, and one where violence was common – a Catholic part of west Belfast. The surprising result was that the greatest control was apparently exercised by the parents in the area of *highest* political violence. Further, it was the boys in this area who were under the greatest parental control compared to the boys in the other two areas. The explanation is that in west Belfast, an area where both the security forces and paramilitary organizations operate, parents wanted to keep a close eye on their sons in particular, in an attempt to secure their physical if not their psychological survival.

Long-term effects: A persistent fear has been that children, either because they have been brought up in atypical circumstances, or perhaps because they have been brought up by harassed parents using unduly authoritarian methods, 'may become a danger to the next generation' if they in turn become parents (Garbarino et al., 1991b). That is, for some the concern is that political violence will impact not just on the child-rearing techniques of the present generation of parents, but will influence the way the next generation of parents will bring up their children.

Most of the evidence that political violence might have a transgenerational impact comes from research on survivors of the Nazi Holocaust and particularly from research on their children. In its weakest form the hypothesis is simply that because of their physical and/or psychological impairments, victims of the Holocaust 'would be less competent as parents and offer less adequate role models' (Sigal and Weinfeld, 1985). More specifically it has been suggested that experiencing the Holocaust led to distortions in the capacity for human relationships and that this in turn produced distortions in parent–child relationships (Sigal, 1973). Hard evidence is difficult to come by in this area. There have been claims however that due to the psychological status of their parents, there has been a 'profound effect' on the children of survivors. One claim has been that these children begin to manifest psychopathology when they reach the age their parents had been when they (the parents) first experienced incarceration (Leon et al., 1981).

In some ways, all of this is rather surprising because, as Nadler et al. (1985) point out, most professionals working in the field have reported that, for survivors, children born after the Holocaust play a tremendously important role, representing as they do a new life and the healing of past traumatic events. For this reason their children tend to be perceived as a source of new hope giving meaning to lives that had been previously shattered. This very observation may be the key to one of the problems that, according to the existing literature, survivor parents have with their children. This problem revolves around the issues of separation and independence (Last, 1988). The suggestion is that survivors, who so often were dramatically separated from their parents, are unable to deal with separation, or impending separation, from their own children. Evidence to back this up comes from a study which involved a non-Jewish control group who were compared with children of survivors. What the pattern of results indicated was that there was a major difference between the comparison group and the children of survivors in the area of independence (Rose and Garake, 1987).

Another suggestion has been that the children of survivors are burdened by their parents' expectations of them (Nadler et al., 1985). In order to avoid inflicting additional pain on their parents these children try to ensure that they do not overtly express aggression towards their parents. As a result, survivors' children are suspected of developing a pattern of repressing aggressive feelings towards their parents, a pattern that is thought to generalize to the rest of society. Nadler et al. (1985), in a study using the Rosenzweig Projective Test, compared children of survivors with matched controls and reported that judges, blind to the hypothesis under test, rated the responses of survivor children as showing more guilt, depression and unexpressed anger. In a follow-up interview the authors gained the impression that the children of survivors were 'burdened by feelings of indebtedness and responsibility towards their parents'. However, in another study Sigal and Weinfeld (1985) reported that a random group of children of survivors, when compared with a control group, showed no effects in the area of control of aggression.

Last (1988), in a review, notes that depression, school problems and excessive quarrelling with siblings have also been cited as characteristic of survivor children although an equal number of studies has found no differences between survivors' children and controls. Last (1988) hints at one reason for these confused findings. He suggests that the contradictory findings that exist in the area have resulted because of the simplistic overgeneralizations that researchers have focused on. These generalizations he notes are the result of the use of unidimensional questions in research. Using a more sophisticated approach he reports finding an interaction between the degree of traumatization of the parent, the gender of the parent and the gender of the child. Finally, it should be noted that we know virtually nothing about the impact on family life when a family member, usually the father, is a combatant but remains in the family home – for example, the many men who engage in secret wars, as members of underground armies. According to McArdle (1949) there was some evidence following World War II that children of French resistance workers caused problems at home. This happened, it is suggested, because these children realized that there was a family secret but resented their exclusion from it and as a result were often aggressive and/or disobedient.

School

The other social institution, along with the family, which plays a major role in the lives of children and young people, is the school. During periods of political violence school systems come under varying degrees of strain depending on the level of violence experienced. For example, during all-out war, as in Europe during the period 1939–45, many things combined to disrupt children's education (McArdle, 1949). Shortages of basic necessities such as fuel for heating, shoes for children's feet or even a shortage of teachers following mass arrests, could all interrupt schooling. Also, the authorities might require children to labour in the fields or parents might require them to search, beg or even steal food.

In less comprehensive wars, for example during the war in Lebanon, the secondary level school population was reported to have declined dramatically as any excuse would do 'for skipping school for days at a time' (Assal and Farrell, 1992). In a similar way, at the beginning of the period of political unrest in Northern Ireland in the early 1970s, the vast majority of schools managed to stay open on a daily basis but did suffer from a marked drop in attendance rates. Rumours at the time claimed that in some schools attendance was down to as low as 50 per cent in the most troubled areas. While this may have been true for some schools on some days official statistics for the whole of Northern Ireland indicated that, in the secondary sector which tended to be most affected, attendance was probably around 70 per cent and after the mid 1970s rose to around 90 per cent.

In other societies it has been common for schools to close for long periods of time. This is what happened in South Africa, for example. Exactly what impact the closing of schools has on the children has not been rigorously investigated and anyway would be difficult to research. According to Usher, one result of school closures in Palestine was the politicizing of children (Usher, 1991). Similarly, Nasson (1986) has noted that in South Africa mass schooling has the potential to equip children for revolt. According to Nasson, therefore, schooling can be at the same time both controlling and liberating. Other observers have claimed that the closing of schools can have a deleterious effect on children because it removes the opportunity to instil in them moral attitudes and values. Certainly, it removes opportunities for educational development.

How much of an impact the breakdown of school has on children will obviously vary from society to society. As Nasson (1986) points out, for many children in South Africa school can not be considered a major influence because half of non-white children drop out of school within four years or less. In other societies, or for other children, disruption of schooling by political violence undoubtedly interferes with educational attainment. Empirical confirmation of this suspicion is available in studies carried out in England following World War II (Titmus, 1950). These studies were based on the results of routine tests given to young men reporting for conscription in the armed services. What these tests revealed was that boys, whose last 2–3 years of school coincided with the highly disrupted conditions of the early years of the war, showed no decline in general intelligence. Despite this, they suffered from a drop in their overall level of educational attainment compared to those who had been at school during the pre-war period. Whether this disruption in educational attainment was due to absence from school, a general drop in standards of teaching or other factors directly impacting on the children themselves is not clear. However, it is interesting to note that Mcfarlane et al. (1987) reporting on the long-term effects of a natural disaster on children in Australia (a bush fire) found a decrease in educational attainment some 8 and 26 months after the disaster had occurred. Further, this report claimed that even mildly symptomatic children were affected. This idea, that stress will influence children's school performance, ties in with the suggestion made by Liddell et al. (1993) that, in South Africa, poverty and stress may interact to increase vulnerability, thus placing at risk young people's potential for educational achievement.

Of course, whether schools manage to maintain their educational standards or not, there is anecdotal evidence from observers in different parts of the world that schools may still play a positive role in the lives of children caught up in political violence. For example Dwork (1991), an historian writing about the lives of Jewish children caught up in the Holocaust notes that in the ghetto children lived on two levels simultaneously. On the one hand they were forced to inhabit an increasingly 'alien and bizarre world'. In coming to terms with this she suggests they struggled to maintain a certain normality and that one of the mediums through which they did this was school. In certain societies it has been maintained that schools act as an 'oasis of peace' in the midst of community violence. This is the claim of a Catholic Bishop in Northern Ireland (Daly, 1989). He contends that in Northern Ireland Catholic teachers and schools (indeed all teachers and schools) have been 'strong factors for stability and normality, at a time when conditions in society brought serious risks of instability and in areas where powerful forces were actively working for destabilization . . .'. Similarly, in the Lebanon Assal and Farrell (1992) noted that children valued school because it brought 'some order to the chaos of their lives' as well as offering protection. In particular, they claim that during periods of heightened stress teachers could have a calming effect on the children.

Play

Psychologists tend to see play as an essential ingredient in the life of children. In particular, it is thought that during play children learn many of the social skills needed to survive in the adult world. The question therefore of what happens to children's play in a society dominated by political violence is an important one. According to Garmezy (1983) there is evidence that while refugee children may recover their general physical health quickly, their social development is more problematic. In particular, he speaks of 'an inability to learn how to play' which marks the behaviour of very young refugee children. Political violence may, therefore, in extreme circumstances, have such an impact on a small number of children.

However, the majority of reports concerning play in societies where political violence is rampant suggest that play does not in fact come to an end. On the contrary, there is evidence that political violence may stimulate children's play. What adults tend to forget perhaps, is that for many children, and indeed for some adults, certain aspects of political violence may actually be stimulating. For example, Smith (1916) reported, perhaps with characteristic English understatement, that 'the first air raid was quite exciting . . . many people rather enjoyed it'. Similarly, Leeson (1917) also noted that World War I 'invoked a spirit of adventure in children', in particular it excited them, especially the boys. Reports from England in World War II appear to confirm this (Gillespie, 1944). Some children, for example, were described as being completely unaffected and indeed were seen to be enjoying 'the new adventure' of being bombed. Therefore, as Garbarino et al. (1991, p. 5) recorded, as a result of their visits to children in many war-torn societies:

> If we are honest we must recognize that war may mean the fun and adventure of being young and set loose on the world. This is one of war's attractions for young people, particularly young people who are trapped in a dead-end existence or who yearn for glory and excitement.

Further, reports from various periods in this century and from various societies indicate not only that political violence may stimulate children's play, but also that the content of such play is likely to mirror the political violence that is going on at that time. For example, there are reports of boys building 'trenches' from snow and throwing sardine tin 'hand grenades' during World War I (Leeson, 1917), while in World War II there are reports of children playing at air raids (Gillespie, 1944). One study carried out in the US in 1943 reported that 'most of the boys owned and played with war toys' and that all but one 'represented war in their play' at school (Geddie and Hildreth, 1944). Nearly 50 years later reports indicate that 'police raid games' were prevalent among children in South Africa (Liddell et al., 1993) while reports from Northern Ireland alleged that children as young as age 4 or 5 years were spending considerable time erecting barricades in their playgroups and pretending to throw petrol bombs.

Reactions to all of this vary. Assal and Farrell (1992) felt that the 'most remarkable part' of their data on play was 'that boys actually played war games'. Other observers have suggested 'that it would be more astonishing if children living in a riot-torn area did not play riot games' (Fraser, 1974). There is also some controversy as to the degree to which children in areas hit by political violence do indulge in play that mimics the adult world around them.

For example, Fields (1973), reporting on children in Northern Ireland, in exactly the same year as Fraser, claims 'they never did play soldier and IRA as they are reported to have done'. Some hard evidence to back up this assertion comes from the study noted above by Liddell et al. (1994) which involved observations of children in four South African communities. These authors recorded the amount of fantasy play which had occurred while the children were being observed. Their observations indicate that less than 10 per cent of the children's fantasy play involved aggression. Further, there was no relationship between aggressive play and aggressive fantasy play. Finally, in all four of the communities studied only a very small amount of the fantasy play was concerned with community violence. What is more, the small amount of fantasy play that could be classified as involving community violence involved almost exclusively things like burglary and theft rather than violence between communities or violence involving the army and/or the police.

These observations are somewhat atypical. Most of the anecdotal evidence indicates that children who experience political violence incorporate this into their play. Empirical confirmation of this observation has been reported by Farver and Frosch (1996) who compared pre-school children who had or had not been directly exposed to the Los Angeles riots of 1992. Narratives were obtained during an individual play sessions. The children who had direct riot exposure were more likely to have aggressive content (hostile and instrumental aggression) in their play narratives and these were more likely to have negative outcomes. Further, in contrast to Liddell et al. (1994), the children who had direct riot exposure made more direct references to riot-specific content.

If these observations are valid they raise the question what role does aggressive play serve in situations of political violence? The most popular explanation is that in war-games children find an opportunity to express their aggressive and destructive impulses 'without excessive guilt' (Despert, 1942), because a violent environment releases taboos against aggression which 'manifest themselves in sadistic phantasies' (Miller, 1940). This fits in with the report by Dawes et al. (1989) that in South Africa play frequently involves the renactment of traumatic events accompanied by 'considerable emotion'. These examples may reinforce Erikson's (1980) claim that play for children 'functions to restore a sense of mastery' and thus enables them to come to terms with their experience of violence.

This is what Punamaki (1993) has concluded as a result of her research with children in Palestine. Play, she suggests (and dreaming) allows children to 'make sense and interpret' their experience in situations of political violence as well as to ventilate emotions. This she claims is possible because in play children can re-enact events and also try out new roles and solutions. Punamaki (1993, p. 8) goes so far as to claim that when political violence has a damaging effect on children's mental health, it is because it has been able to 'prevent, intrude upon and distort the healing function of play . . .'.

Others, for example Usher (1991), see play among children in politically-violent societies as having a more political significance. In particular, it has been suggested that the games Palestinian children play provide 'the ideological cement from which the child's national identity is forged'. According to Usher (1991, p. 10) play is not simply the reliving of common experiences, rather, 'it is the collective means by which children recover, internalize and identify with past and contemporary Palestinian reality'.

Whatever the developmental significance of the content of play in politically-violent societies and the psychological motivation underlying it, there is little doubt that in these societies play outside the home exposes children to considerable physical danger. One reason for this is that at such times there is likely to be less adult supervision: there may be no parents around, fathers may be away fighting or possibly in detention, and mothers may either be working or overstretched at home. In addition, there is likely to be less schooling or less pressure to attend school. As a result of such factors, according to Titmus (1950) during the period 1940–43 in England an additional 756 children aged up to fifteen were drowned, not while swimming in the sea or in swimming pools, but in sewage tanks, wells and the large emergency water tanks that the fire service positioned in inner-city areas. In many parts of the world today the number of children missing lower limbs testifies to the fact that play for children in areas where landmines have been used, perhaps in a conflict now resolved, is an exceptionally dangerous activity.

Aggression

According to Punamaki (1987) the hostility, destructiveness, and aggression of war can never be thought of as simply an external stress for children. Rather it inevitably becomes part of the child's inner fantasy life and world of emotions. In reaching this conclusion, she was very much influenced by the work of Freud and Burlingham. These two psychoanalytically-oriented researchers had reported extensively on the development of pre-school children in England during World War II. According to Freud and Burlingham (1943) destructive and aggressive impulses, which were in the process of being repressed in the young children they studied, were easily aroused by the overt aggression in the world around them.

Yet this is not what Rautman and Brower (1945) found when they studied children in the US in 1943. These elementary-school children were asked to make up a story in response to ten pictures from the Thematic Apperception Test. These stories were then analysed for mention of the war, killing and death. What Rautman and Brower found was that only some 40 per cent even mentioned the war, and an even smaller proportion (6 per cent) of all stories actually had a 'frank war theme'. At every age level more boys' than girls' stories had an overt war theme and this proportion tended to increase with increasing age. A similar proportion of stories also mentioned death (5 per cent) or killing (6 per cent).

This study is of interest for two reasons. To begin with, it suggests that only a small proportion of these children, growing up in a nation which was one of the leading protagonists in a world war, could be said to be in any way preoccupied with the war or with death or killing.

The second reason that this study is of interest is that it was repeated some seven years later in 1950 with children from exactly the same schools in the same US city and employing exactly the same methodology (Rautman and Brower, 1951). This time, not surprisingly, the proportion of children mentioning war had dropped from 30 to 16 per cent while stories employing an overtly war-related theme also fell from 6 to 2 per cent. However, what was remarkable was that the proportion of stories mentioning death or killing remained at approximately the same level in 1950 as in 1943. As the authors concluded (p. 269)

> War as a factor in children's thinking thus seems to vary with the times, but death and killing by one means or another appear to be constant features of even a young child's life

Of course, this information comes from children who had not been directly exposed to political violence. Information on children who had been directly exposed comes from a study by Punamaki (1987) which involved Israeli and Arab children – some of the latter living on the West Bank. Using the Rosenzweig Picture Frustration test Punamaki reported that both Israeli and Palestinian children showed roughly the same amount of aggression. She also reported that fear and anxiety were as common in response to frustrating situations as was aggression. In view of the fact that some of the Arab children in her study, those living on the West Bank had been more overtly exposed to war, it would seem that these results do not support the earlier speculation regarding the impact of political violence on children's levels of aggression. It has to be added that the absence of any comparable data from a control group outside of the Middle East makes these results difficult to interpret. Also, neither Punamaki's study nor those noted earlier by Brower and Rautman focused on children's behaviour.

More relevant information is available in a study reported by Dawes et al. (1989). In this study, parents in a South African squatter community that had been attacked and burnt to the ground, were asked to report difficulties that they had with their children aged 2–17 years. What is obvious from the graphical display of the data presented by Dawes and his colleagues is that social difficulties, which included aggression plus shyness, were among the problems least frequently reported by all parents. Less than 5 per cent reported a problem in this area.

Social problems were, however, most frequently reported by the parents of 7–11 year olds. Among boys in this age group in particular some 10 per cent of parents reported such problems. According to Dawes et al. (1989) these problems took the form either of aggressive interactions with peers or very little interaction at all. Again, the evidence is difficult to interpret. It does, however, make it seem unlikely that one can agree with Punamaki (1987) that in children exposed to political violence identification with combatants means that a 'warlike and aggressive manner' becomes the 'principal feature of the child's personality'.

Better data are available in a study carried out by Chiemienti, Nasr and Khalifeh (1989) in the Lebanon. This involved a random sample of approximately 1,000 children aged 3–9 years. These children were classified as coming from a family that had either experienced trauma (about 30 per cent of the total sample) or not. The trauma included such things as displacement of the family or destruction of the home or the death of a family member. Mothers were asked to complete a check-list that included, among other things, several forms of behaviour which could be subsumed under the heading of aggression – e.g. shouting/screaming, hitting/kicking/destroying objects, hurting verbally or physically or 'trouble-making'. What the results of this study revealed was that significantly more mothers from the 'traumatized' families were likely to report that their children exhibited these behaviours. Among the aggressive behaviours, shouting/screaming were the most common, being reported by 63 per cent of the mothers from the 'traumatized' families and 45 per cent from the non-'traumatized' families. The rates for hitting/kicking were 38 per cent and 23 per cent respectively while the remaining behaviours were reported by about 20 per cent of the mothers from the 'traumatized' families and around 10 per cent of the non-'traumatized' group. Only the behaviour of destroying objects did not discriminate between the children from the 'traumatized' and the non-'traumatized' families. In addition certain behaviours were more common among boys – in particular hurting physically. Destroying objects was more common among the younger 3–6 year-old age group; among the older 7–9 year age group hurting verbally was more common.

On the basis of these results, Chiemienti et al. (1989) suggest that the most likely explanation for this increased aggression among children in situations of political violence is some form of modelling. Such children they note are exposed repeatedly 'at an age of high susceptibility to familiar real-life aggressive models who are rewarded with recognition, status and privileges'.

A similar conclusion, though posed in less dramatic terms, was reached by Liddell et al. (1994). They present even more convincing evidence that young children's levels of aggression may be influenced by their exposure to political violence. In the literature on children and political violence this study is unusual in many ways. To begin with, it is one of the few studies to use direct observations of children as opposed to parental ratings or questionnaires. Secondly, it involved relatively young children, 5-year olds. Finally, it focused on children who, while living in a society in which political violence was rife, were not living in communities in which political violence was a dominant feature of everyday life – in contrast to, for example, the children in the study from the Lebanon reviewed earlier.

The children lived in four South African townships which were rated on a violence scale from low violence to high violence. All 80 children were followed and observed during a total of 1,440 30-second observation periods per child. In addition biographical and socio-economic data were also collected.

The results suggested that the children living in the more violent communities were slightly more aggressive. It is important to note, however, that overall levels of aggression were very low. Children on average spent only some 0.5 per cent of the time observed engaged in aggressive behaviours, which is less than 4 minutes of the 12 hours during which they were observed. As Liddell and her colleagues (1994) point out, there was therefore no evidence to suggest that aggression had reached anything like pathological levels among these children.

Because of the detailed nature of the information gathered in this study the authors were able to say that the main cause of aggressive behaviour was failure to co-operate during a game or fantasy episode. What is particularly interesting is that it was also possible to demonstrate that, although the children from the more violent communities displayed more aggression, children in all communities expressed aggression in much the same contexts.

Finally, the authors were able to show that the level of aggression shown by the children was most influenced by the amount of contact they had with older boys and men, although aggressive episodes themselves almost always involved same-aged partners. As a result, Liddell and her colleagues (1994) concluded that modelling and imitation probably played a major role in determining the amount of aggression shown by the 5 year-old children in their study.

This study is of particular importance because it illustrates that the impact of political violence in certain societies may not be as dramatic as has been hypothesized in the past. Despite this, political violence may still have a real impact on children's behaviour even if the effect is much more subtle than earlier commentators had believed.

Liddell et al.'s study is also significant for several methodological reasons. To begin with in an area that is marked by speculation it represents one of the few attempts to test empirically a hypothesis that has existed for many years.

In addition, Liddell et al.'s paper is an illustration of how excellent research can be undertaken in difficult circumstances. In particular, it demonstrates that it takes time and care to research the more subtle effects of political violence.

Also their work introduces a methodological approach that has been almost totally absent from the literature on children and political violence – that of direct observation. In particular it illustrates the importance of research that employs ecologically valid methods. Finally this study illustrates the optimum way in which outsider and insider can collaborate as researchers to the best effect, which is again a phenomenon not common in the literature.

Aggression as Coping

The idea that modelling can explain increased aggression among children exposed to political violence, a suggestion made in both the Chiemienti and Liddell studies, is of particular interest. This is because it runs counter to the suggestion, that aggression may be thought of as a coping mechanism, which is beginning to emerge as the results of a series of epidemiological studies in Northern Ireland (Fee, 1980, 1983; McGrath and Wilson, 1985; McWhirter, 1983).

The first series of these studies used the teacher-based Rutter Scale, while McWhirter's study employed a self-rating instrument, the Junior Eysenck Personality Questionnaire (JEPQ). As noted in chapter 2, around 10 per cent of children in Northern Ireland tend to score above the cut-off point on the Rutter Scale, which is not a startlingly high figure, but is somewhat above what has been found in comparable samples in other societies. More interesting information has emerged when the subscales from the Rutter have been examined separately. This has shown that there is agreement across the different surveys because it is the subscale which taps antisocial and acting-out behaviour, and conduct disorder, which always accounts for the higher scores. What is more, this result parallels McWhirter's finding that Northern Irish children had relatively high Psychoticism scores on the JEPQ because it is the Psychoticism subscale that taps antisocial behaviour. In addition, all these studies are in agreement that these findings apply mainly to boys.

These reports from Northern Ireland, of increased antisocial/aggressive behaviour among the young, are of particular interest because they come from a society in which there has not been a marked increase in the proportion of young people diagnosed as clinically ill (see chapter 2) or being brought before the courts. It can be concluded therefore that while there may be an increase in aggression among young people in Northern Ireland as a result of political violence, this is a fairly subtle effect of concern to teachers perhaps and possibly to the children themselves – but not to psychiatrists or magistrates.

There are of course several possible explanations for this increased level of antisocial/aggressive behaviour, modelling being the most obvious. However, researchers in Northern Ireland have tended to reject this possibility. Instead, they have opted for a possible link between psycho-social stress and aggressive motivations by choosing to regard aggression as a type of coping response (Wilson and Cairns, 1993). For example, Fee (1980, p. 41) speculated that the elevated Rutter Scale scores he found in Northern Ireland may have been brought about because the violence 'caused neurotic behaviour to be displaced by antisocial behaviour'. Taking the idea further, McWhirter (1983) remarked, 'the young lad who has grown up in a ghetto where the norm is stone-throwing against the British Army or against the other side, and where paramilitary activity is rife, may not end up a neurotic but he may end up a terrorist'.

This is not a new idea, and this suggestion is not confined to Northern Ireland. Despert (1942) was perhaps the first to suggest that aggression, in which she included delinquency, may be a defence mechanism against anxiety. More recently, in South Africa, Thomas (1990) has suggested that for township children subjected to humiliation and brutalization 'violence can often be a way of relieving . . . stress'.

Of course, as Wilson and Cairns (1993) have pointed out, it is difficult to disentangle the relationship between political violence and behavioural disturbance in young people from the possible confounding effects of socio-economic disadvantage, given that these two sources of stress tend to co-vary. Indeed, the possibility that the negative effect induced by either may bring about aggression and hostility is supported by research on adolescent emotional development, which has shown that the negative effect, particularly in boys, is often expressed as hostility, aggression and conduct disturbance (Sroufe and Rutter, 1984). As Wilson and Cairns (1993) note, these ideas fit well with Berkowitz's (1990) neo-associationist model of aggression which suggests that aversive environments generate the negative effect. In turn, this may either be internalized or externalized, according to the coping responses of the affected person. If the latter occurs 'negative effect is the basic source of anger and angry aggression' (Berkowitz, 1990, p. 494).

Moral Development

It has been hypothesized by Garbarino et al. (1991b) that children in societies where political violence exists develop an 'enhanced capacity to see the world with sensitivity and moral astuteness'. This would suggest that living in the midst of political violence can accelerate moral development. This is a unique view, however. It appears to be more generally accepted in the literature that children's socialization in societies experiencing political violence will prove to be problematic. This is so, according to Punamaki (1987, p. 33), because in such societies 'children cannot be successfully socialized . . . in a period when the behaviour of their whole society is based on . . . the denial of human values'.

This concern for moral development in societies where political violence is common has usually taken one of two forms. To begin with, there is the vague fear that living in such a society will lead to 'the truncation' of moral development in whole generations (Fields, 1973). A second concern has been that either consequent on the truncation of moral reasoning, or for other reasons, there will be a reduction in actual standards of behaviour among the young. Lower levels of moral behaviour, it is often claimed, are reflected in a rise in levels of crime among young people, a general increase in antisocial, especially aggressive, behaviour and an overall lessening of respect for authority figures in society such as the police, teachers and indeed adults in general.

Moral Reasoning

The proposition that children's general moral development, as measured by traditional tests of moral reasoning, may be influenced by living in the midst of on-going political violence appears to have been tested in one society only – Northern Ireland. And according to Cairns (1987) there is some patchy evidence from Northern Ireland to support this prediction. What this evidence suggests is that compared to their peers in England or in the United States (but not in the Republic of Ireland) Northern Irish children and young people are more likely to perform at a lower level on objective tests of moral reasoning. For example, Breslin (1982) in a large study involving 17 year olds claimed that only 28 per cent could be classified at the principled state of moral development. Similarly, both Kahn (1982) using the Defining Issues Test and Cairns and Conlon (1985) using the Sociomoral Reflection Objective Measure found that Irish children on average scored at a lower level compared to their North American peers. In particular, there is a suggestion that 'Northern Irish young people are not so aware of the complexity of moral problems' (Cairns, 1987).

These results are interesting because Garbarino and Bronfenbrenner (1976) have suggested that different types of environments/societies encourage the development of different types of morality. In an anomic setting, according to their model, only the lowest (self-oriented) level of moral development is likely to be reached – Level 0 in terms of Kohlberg's stages. In monolithic settings where social agents are organized around a single set of goals a pattern of morality develops where allegiance to a system of social agents is most likely to dominate. This corresponds roughly to Kholberg's levels I–IV.

According to Garbarino and Bronfenbrenner only in pluralistic settings 'in which social agents and entities represent somewhat different expectations, sanctions, and rewards for members of society' are children given the 'opportunity, security and social support for the development of abstract thinking and speculation as a consequence of partially competing and overlapping social allegiances'. Thus, only in such an environment are children likely to reach the 'highest' level of moral development equivalent to Kholberg's level V.

This model may provide a useful way to think about moral development in Northern Ireland and perhaps also in South Africa. In particular, the suggestion is that despite the continuing political violence Northern Ireland has not turned into an anomic society and there is no evidence that its children have become totally amoral. There is, on the other hand, evidence that Northern Ireland is a society that can be thought of as a monolithic. It could be argued that two monoliths exist built around the two respective church-based communities, both of which command a high degree of loyalty and with which most people in Northern Ireland identify (Cairns, 1982). In such a society, as noted above, Garbarino and Bronfenbrenner's model would predict that moral reasoning would develop, but would fail to reach the highest or principled level. This is exactly what the few empirical studies that have been carried out appear to indicate.

If children in Northern Ireland are indeed 'retarded' (Fields, 1973) in terms of moral reasoning then one might also expect them to show less respect for authority. In the general psychological literature on moral development however, there is still controversy as to the possibility of a clear link between moral reasoning and behaviour (Ress, Bebeau and Volker, 1986 cited in Dawes 1992). This means that evidence that children exhibit lower levels of moral reasoning does not automatically mean that they also exhibit lower levels of moral behaviour.

Therefore it should not be surprising that two studies in Northern Ireland have failed to provide evidence that children in Northern Ireland are more approving of violence, either in interpersonal or more social settings. In the first of these studies (Cairns, 1983) some 600 children were asked to respond to a series of situations typical of those children might find themselves in at school or with friends. For example, 'a boy is playing a game and keeps making mistakes, another boy starts making fun of him'. The children were then invited to suggest first how most boys would respond in this situation and, secondly, how the boy should respond to this situation. The possible responses were either 'physical aggression', 'verbal aggression', 'leaving the field' or 'positive coping'. What this study demonstrated was that whether the children involved lived in a high violence area in Northern Ireland, or in a low violence area or indeed in the Republic of Ireland, where there is no political violence, they were agreed as to what the correct levels of violence were for each situation. In other words, it appeared that exposure to political violence had not altered their ideas about the morality of violence in the classroom or in the playground.

The second study, by Lorenc and Branthwaite (1986), was also not able to provide any support for the idea that children in Northern Ireland are more approving or tolerant of violence, this time either from or to authority figures. This study was based not on actual behaviour but on the responses given by boys and girls of 10–11 years old to various scenarios which involved violence to or from parents/teachers or the security forces (police/soldiers). The children were asked to rate each scenario on a five-point scale from 'not wrong at all' to 'very wrong indeed'. The children came from a relatively high violence area in Northern Ireland. The results of this study suggested that compared to English children of the same age, Northern Irish children were, if anything, more inclined to judge violent acts as wrong.

Crime

On the other hand, claims linking increased political violence to an increase in amoral behaviour among young people have been common in this century. One example is Geiger (1968,

p. 7) writing about the Russian revolution during which, he notes, young people, apparently abandoned by their families became 'a public menace, roaming the streets in gangs and committing every crime and violent act'. Observing the phenomenon is one thing. Establishing that it is definitely caused by on-going political violence is more difficult. Part of the problem is that societies in the past did not keep proper statistics. Even in today's societies embroiled in political violence official statistics, as noted earlier, are often inadequate or non-existent. However, in this century at least three cases exist where official statistics were maintained despite on-going violence.

Britain: World War I: One of the earliest and most comprehensive attempts to look at the claim that an increase in political violence leads to a change in the moral climate of society which is in turn reflected in crime among young people was the report prepared by Cecil Leeson for The Howard Association in 1917, written in England when the World War I was at its height. According to this report figures were available to show that during the war there occurred a 'grave increase in the number of juvenile offenders, and especially of juvenile thieves'. This increase in crime among young people apparently was mainly confined to boys and was not confined to any one geographical area.

According to Leeson, the official figures represented only the tip of the iceberg. Or as he put it ' for every thousand children who succumb to the unwholesome conditions . . . the lives of many thousands more will carry the impress of those conditions' (p. 10). Leeson was apparently in no doubt that this increase in crime among young boys was a direct reflection of the conditions under which children were forced to live at this time. These conditions, according to him, precluded healthy moral growth. In his extensive report he was at some pains to outline the various reasons why this increase in juvenile crime may have occurred, an increase incidentally which took place at a time when crime among adults was actually falling.

One of the prime causes he hypothesized was the 'spirit of adventure' which infected children at that time. Children, he noted, were used to hearing from their friends and relatives 'thrilling accounts of trench warfare'. According to Leeson, therefore, what would now be referred to as modelling played an important part in children's involvement in crime. A second major cause he suggested was that during the war adults were simply too busy to devote enough time to children. This Leeson noted was evident in such obvious things as the fact that there were many fewer policemen on duty, the war having placed extra demands on the police manpower. Among those adults who were left at home there was not the same time or energy left to devote to such things as youth clubs or even school work. In the home, father was often away, in the army, or on essential war work. Mothers were also often employed in such places as munitions factories where they replaced the men who were absent on military service. All of this he maintains led to a breakdown in family life and in particular to poor attendance at school.

Britain: World War II: Despite the fact that the increase in juvenile crime had been well documented during World War I the people of Britain appear to have been taken by surprise when a similar phenomenon appeared during World War II. Again, this ran counter to many other statistics as Titmus (1950, p. 340), writing in the official report on the effects of World War II on the civilian population, notes:

> there was no evidence of an increase in insanity, the number of suicides fell, the statistics of drunkenness went down by more than half, there was much less disorderly behaviour in the streets and public places, . . . only the juvenile delinquency figures registered a rise.

This time, however, there was some disagreement among the experts as to whether this was clearly an effect of the war. One claim was, that the increase in juvenile crime which came to public notice during the first years of the war, was actually a trend which had first begun during the mid 1930s (Crosby, 1986).

However, the consensus appears to be that in 1940 and 1941

in particular, there was a genuine increase in crime among young people (Lewis, 1942). A Home Office and Board of Education circular in June 1941 claimed that the returns for the first 12 months of the war, compared with the previous 12 months, indicated an increase in the whole country of 41 per cent in the number of children under 14 years found guilty of indictable offences and an increase of 22 per cent in the age-group 14–17 years. These increases coincided roughly with the period during which air raids were at their height. Despite this it was claimed that this was a general phenomenon and was not confined just to those areas that had suffered from bombing (Vernon, 1941).

Most contemporary commentators suggested (for example, Bodman and Dundson, 1941) that this increase in crime was due to such things as a lower level of supervision at home and disorganization of the school system due to bombing and/or evacuation. Other interesting explanations were, however, also entertained. For example Pritchard and Rosenzweig (1942) suggested that the increase in crime among young people was related not simply to the crumbling social structure of the world in which young people found themselves at that time but more precisely to the fact that this created within children 'a deep latent anxiety'. As a means of overcoming this anxiety, and filling the vacuum left by adults, boys in particular sought the security of gangs. The organization of gangs in turn facilitated criminal activities. (A somewhat similar claim has been made with regard to children joining terrorist groups – see chapter 4).

Titmus (1950, p. 340) however has a different perspective. He suggests that the increase in the proportion of children involved in crime was more a reflection of the effect of the war on adults, rather than of the effects of the war on children. To back up this claim he noted that

> the proportion of boys under fourteen years who were ordered corporal punishment for offences of various kinds by magistrates, which was falling before the war, rose during the two years of bombing (1940–1) by over six hundred per cent. Thereafter, the proportion declined rapidly.

Titmus, commenting on 'these glimpses of the moral effects of a nation conducting war' suggests that the increased birching of more little boys may have been more a reflection of the 'aspirations and prejudices of the moment'!

Northern Ireland: Given this general background it is perhaps not surprising that some twenty years later when political conflict began to develop on a large scale in Northern Ireland the authorities were gripped, according to Caul (1983) with something resembling 'moral panic'. Apparently, the expectation in government circles was that the increase in juvenile crime would be such as to swamp the existing specialist services in this area. However, what actually occurred, much to the surprise presumably of many experts at that time in Northern Ireland, was that the official statistics for the period 1968–72 actually revealed a dramatic decrease in the number of crimes committed by young people. Rather than welcoming these facts the authorities apparently interpreted these as being due to the preoccupation of the police with other more serious events in Northern Ireland at the time. They therefore feared a resurgence of crime among young people when Northern Ireland returned to more normal life.

Other explanations for the low rate of crime among young people in Northern Ireland were low detection rates on the part of the police (Curran, 1984) or a large proportion of unreported crime. Another possibility (Caul, 1983) was the existence of an alternative justice system in some parts of Northern Ireland provided by paramilitary organizations. Known to hand out rough justice from their kangaroo courts in the form of 'knee-cappings', such organizations, it was claimed, may also have had an impact on reported crime. Heskin (1981) has however argued that the amount of unreported crime in Northern Ireland was no more or less than in other parts of England and Wales. He therefore concluded that the proportion of young people involved in crime in Northern Ireland was substantially lower than in other parts of the United Kingdom. The general conclusion has been therefore that the increase in crime due to the troubles has actually stabilized at quite a low level.

All of these studies have several features in common, though they cover a time span of some 60–70 years and involve conflicts varying in form and intensity. In particular, there is little to support the notion that political violence has a *direct* impact on the amount of crime committed by young people. Rather, all three appear to suggest that secondary causes such as adult supervision and in particular the amount of time that the authorities have to devote to detecting crime carried out by young people are important factors.

Europe: 1939–45: Of course, in none of these societies just discussed could it be said that political violence ever reached a level where the normal functions of society totally disintegrated. As this disentegration takes place the line that divides criminal activity from political activity on the part of young people becomes almost imperceptible. For example in parts of South Africa it has been observed that young people involved in politically-motivated violence are much more likely to be involved in conventional crime (Liddell et al., 1993). The problem for researchers is that as political violence intensifies on a local level, not only is a functioning police service likely to disappear, but also no one is left who bothers to keep the statistics on juvenile crime. In such societies it then becomes impossible to try to estimate the role of political violence as a causal factor in juvenile crime.

Such was the state of affairs in most of the countries of mainland Europe from 1939–45. For most of these countries, at that time occupied by a foreign power, it was not until the war ended that they began to take stock of the impact this episode in their history had had on their young people. And certainly, at the end of the war, as the allied armies moved across Europe, it appeared to many that moral standards had disintegrated entirely, with, 'at that time, a whole new underworld of beggary and lawlessness . . . [plus] . . . every kind and degree of juvenile delinquency . . . from mere childish defiance to prostitution and organized crime' (McArdle, 1949, p. 260).

Much of this was, of course, blamed on the fact that these children had been growing up in occupied countries. This was in itself considered to be a stimulus to lawlessness. As McArdle (1949, p. 262) points out, for many children in occupied Europe it was a duty to break laws:

> to crash through regulations, to lie, to trick to deceive, to carry out sabotage, to create confusion, to work as badly and as slowly as possible, to set fire to stores – these things were things that it had become brave and admirable to do.

So great was the concern for juvenile delinquency in Europe at the end of the war that a special conference was held in Geneva in 1947 which was attended by delegates from most European countries (International Child Welfare Review, 1947). This conference was called to try to get the facts, according to the organizers, given that juvenile delinquency was a topic 'which public imagination is apt to distort'.

In general the delegates were cautious about interpreting the limited data available to them. Doubts about the accuracy of the statistics were quelled to some extent, however, by the remarkable similarity of trends across nations. These trends indicated that virtually every country had experienced an increase in juvenile crime during the war – surprisingly including Switzerland which remained officially neutral. In addition, it was agreed that while the graph was somewhat similar to that for juvenile crime during World War I, this time the increase was on a much larger scale.

One clue to what had actually taken place lay in the fact that the number of *types* of crime had not increased. Rather, the increase was mainly in offences against property, especially theft. The conference concluded, therefore, that:

> the war did not make people more sanguinary, sadistic, shameless or crooked. It tripled the number of thefts, the rise being largely due to minors following the example of their elders, who took by stealing what they could not get in normal pre-war ways. What collapsed therefore was not so much respect for persons, nor even respect for authority, as respect for other people's property. (International Child Welfare Review, 1947, p. 74)

Such was the widespread involvement in petty theft that the representative from the Netherlands noted that in his country 'this war had been a lesson in humility' for those who before the war had looked down on delinquents.

In general then the conference recognized that there had been an increase in juvenile delinquency, but that this was mostly due to economic difficulties, the general disorganization of social life and the consequent breaking up of family life.

Long-term effects: An important question, was, of course, is the effect short-term or long-term? An optimistic answer was provided by the Austrian delegation who reported data from Austria for the period 1919–38. This analysis followed crime rates per thousand for two cohorts – one born in the period 1904–8, and the other born in the period 1909–18.

The results showed that the first cohort, who were more open to the influences of World War I, committed more crimes from ages 14–19 years. By the time both cohorts had reached the age of 24–25 years, however, the figures were virtually identical. The authors therefore concluded that 'there were not more habitual thieves' in the first group than in the second. This study thus appears to confirm what other delegates had suspected, that children who become delinquent in a period of exceptional national crisis do not show any increased tendency towards crime when they reach adulthood.

This idea that children's moral standards are situationally dependent is important and linked to the suggestion by Emler (1984) that a young person's moral standards are likely to be influenced by his/her social identity. This means that violent behaviour will not automatically generalize to another setting as Fraser (1974) suggested. Instead, whether this will happen or not will depend on the social identity switched on by a particular social situation (Dawes, 1992). This in turn is a problem which is very closely related to the main topic of the next chapter, the relationship between growing up in a politically violent society, and involvement in politics and violence.

Summary

The 'normal' problems that children face during childhood do not evaporate simply because of the onset of political violence, in particular the disadvantages associated with lower socioeconomic status. Even for children in societies where there is political violence these may still be the major hurdles of everyday life. In addition, because political violence can damage the general infrastructure of society, for example disrupting medical services or the food supply, children may be exposed to many risks other than the obvious problems of dealing with bombs and bullets, including increased risk of accidental injury or death. These conclusions are based on good evidence; further evidence is also now becoming available to suggest that it is likely that there is a cumulative effect with the direct negative consequences of political violence added to the effects of economic and social disadvantage.

Part of this increased risk may be due, it has been suggested, to the fact that the whole family structure comes under stress as a result of political violence. In particular this may include changes in child-rearing tactics. Further there is speculation that these changes may carry over to influence the way in which the next generation bring up their children. Unfortunately despite the importance of this area the amount of hard evidence is almost negligible. Only the speculation that changes in child-rearing styles accompany exposure to political violence has really been tested and even then only in a very limited way.

Anecdotal evidence suggests that where schools can be kept open they may act as to protect children but this need to be confirmed empirically. On the other hand, it is clear that political violence can and often does disrupt schooling, either because children do not attend school or because schools are forced to close. The evidence for this is reliable but is confined to developed societies. This may be because schooling is an issue that is more likely to be important in developed countries, or perhaps statistics are more readily available there. Whatever the reason more research is needed in less developed societies on this topic.

Whether or not families, or schools, are able to fulfil their usual roles, children still need to play. And what is clear is that exposure to political violence can be exciting for children, contrary to the impression given by some adults who tend to think of it only in negative terms. On the other hand it is true that such play may well involve actual physical danger for children.

Also many adult observers claim to see in children's play at these times the reproduction of the aggressive behaviour of the adult world. This is a claim that has been subjected to empirical scrutiny but with contrasting results. Therefore, while there is no doubt that play exposes children to dangers, whether its content is greatly influenced by ongoing political violence is open to question. At the moment there is good evidence for both positions.

Adult observers have in turn tended to link increased aggression in play with increased aggression in everday life. Either because children are modelling themselves on the adults around them or because aggressive behaviour is a form of coping, the expectation has been that exposure to political violence will lead to an increase in aggressive behaviour, for example when interacting with peers.

At least two well-designed studies have examined this question and each has reached a different conclusion. The first of these (Chiementi et al., 1989) claimed to have found a marked relationship while the second (Liddell et al., 1994) found the relationship to be much more subtle.

Evaluating the evidence is difficult because no two studies were exactly the same. Two studies involved children exposed to long-term political violence but only one of these employed observational methods. In the third study the children were observed but had only been exposed to political violence for a short time. Therefore despite the unusually high quality of the evidence, no clear conclusions can be reached. If nothing else, this illustrates the urgent need for cross-national replication of research in this area.

Despite much speculation that children's moral attitudes and values may be altered by exposure to political violence there is little empirical evidence to confirm this hypothesis. What evidence there is appears to come almost exclusively from one society – Northern Ireland. The suggestion is that children in Northern Ireland may have an underdeveloped sense of the complexity of moral problems. This comes from research using measures of moral reasoning. However, when moral behaviour (measured using paper and pencil tests) has been examined, no effect for political violence has been found.

Some of these results are of particular interest because they may fit the theoretical ideas of Garbarino and Bronfenbrenner (1976). On the other hand, the evidence is somewhat patchy and needs to be confirmed in other societies before it can be accepted.

Whatever the explanation, permanent changes in morality are almost certainly not linked to an increase in crime among young people at this time. Juvenile crime does increase with increasing political violence but the most likely explanation for this is the absence of authority figures such as fathers or the police combined with extreme levels of deprivation. The evidence also suggests that long-term effects in this area are probably minimal. This is an area where by the standard of the field the evidence is adequate. Again, however, it has been confined to the developed world. What it appears to illustrate once again is that the moral panic experienced by adults when children are exposed to political violence is not backed up by hard data.

4 Children as Political Activists

A young generation is in the making which will be part of the community, belonging to it and nothing else. This generation will realize and fulfil things which today we can only prophesize and see in our dreams.

Speech by Adolph Hitler, Munich, February 1935

The rise of the Nazi movement is one of the most remarkable and frightening political phenomena of this century. For the most part Nazis were created in one generation by adults who used their knowledge of national traditions to mould a whole generation of young people to serve their evil ends. It is correct to say, therefore, that Hitler's first victims were the children of Germany who 'fired to a white heat of devotion . . . were then hammered and twisted like iron on the anvil into weapons for his ends' (McArdle, 1949, p. 19).

The tools that Hitler used to create this weapon of war were such that although the Hitler Youth was only formed in 1926, by the end of 1935 there were groups in 53 countries as well as in the homeland, and membership, at its height, has been estimated at six million. Throughout all of this the Nazis put a major emphasis on the training of young boys. This process began as early as six years, and for those who went on through the ranks, was not completed until their early twenties.

Few children escaped this training and contemporary records

suggest that only a minority wanted to do so. Indeed, reports from occupied countries such as Holland and Belgium (International Child Welfare Review, 1947) indicated that even young children from homes where the family remained loyal to the pre-occupation government became embroiled to the point where they were charged with 'political offences' in the post-war period. Other observers in these countries reported cases of children joining the Waffen SS at age 17 years (the minimum age) against the wishes of their parents.

Hitler achieved all this by gaining complete control of the educational system including teacher training, requiring teachers to swear an oath to train children in Nazi ideology and even taking over their professional organizations. As a result school books were changed to support the Nazi creed while the radio, press, plays and movies were all harnessed to carry the same message, with no counter-suggestions allowed to intrude.

What we today appear to have failed to learn from this phenomenon, or have learned but forgotten, is that in certain circumstances, particularly where they feel their historical and deeply-rooted identities threatened, young people can come to

> support doctrines offering a total immersion in a synthetic identity (extreme nationalism, racism or class consciousness) . . . [such] . . . indoctrination contributes significantly to that mixture of righteousness and criminality which, under totalitarian conditions, becomes available for organized terror and/or the establishment of major industries of extermination. (Erikson, 1964, p. 93)

Passive Victims?

Despite this vivid example from the relatively recent past, the literature concerned with children in societies where political violence exists today tends to see children as relatively passive victims. However, from a number of societies evidence is available that far from being passive onlookers to the political struggles in their country children may be 'channelling their energies politically' (Chikane, 1986) and in so doing they may develop an 'astute and intense political consciousness' (Usher, 1991). These two observations, from South Africa and Palestine, respectively, illustrate situations where children have not simply been passive victims of political violence, but instead have played an active part in the on-going political struggles in their society.

Gibson (1991) suggests it is a mistake to believe that children in such settings lack political knowledge. Her observations in South Africa have led her to believe that children's political ideas are 'fundamental in moulding their psychological response to violence'. In South Africa, she claims, children come to appreciate the political meaning of violence at an early age and that these ideas are well integrated into their political beliefs by adolescence. Similarly, in Palestine, Darweish (1989) contends that the generation we have watched on our television screens daily confronting Israeli soldiers has, because of this active participation in political violence, had its political understanding 'sharpened'. As a result these young people are 'familiar with current political arguments and have a political affiliation with a particular ideology within the PLO'.

Not everyone agrees with this conclusion however. Fields (1973), based on her experience in Northern Ireland, claimed that 'violence and terrorism do not politicize growing children, they turn instead to taking violent action – not toward political measures'. Obviously therefore, not everyone is convinced that active involvement can be equated with politicization. In general, the psychological literature has claimed that children, especially younger children, tend to take a relatively authoritarian view of the world and thus come to idealize political phenomena. Echoes of this have been hinted at by observers of children who have become actively involved with political violence. For example, young Palestinians, it has been claimed, 'tend to understand politics as black or white, good or bad, friend or enemies' (Kuttab, 1998). Similarly, Woods (1989) has maintained that in South Africa most of the youths involved in the political struggles have only a sketchy notion of the political ideology underlying their actions.

The important point here is that these are empirical questions. In other words, it cannot be assumed that (violent) political action is based on ideological commitment. It is equally possible that it is involvement in political violence which leads to the development of ideological commitment. In his study of the young communists and storm-troopers who were politically active in Germany in the 1930s, Merkle (1986) concluded that if anything, the latter is a more likely explanation. Their confrontations, he suggests, had more to do with 'aroused emotions, brawny fists . . . than with ideological concepts' (Merkle, 1986). Similarily, in war-time Holland, it was claimed that only 5–7 per cent of young Nazis consciously adopted the Nazi ideology. The remainder had no political opinions but 'merely absorbed undigested notions' (International Child Welfare Review, 1947). According to Merkle therefore, for many activists 'ideology continues to be a rather irrelevant and unnecessary preoccupation of some of their comrades and leaders'. In this respect it may be important to understand that, as Woods (1989) has noted, based on observations in South Africa, only a small proportion of young people in a neighbourhood – he suggests less than 5 per cent – is needed to impose a political identity on a community unchallenged.

Nevertheless, what has tended to fascinate journalists and television cameramen in particular is that in many societies where political violence can be found children can also be found taking an active part. The roles these children adopt can vary from what is in effect an extension of the kind of gang culture found in many societies to forced service as child-soldiers with many variations in between. In an attempt to understand the nature of children's active involvement in political violence this chapter will examine first the nature of that involvement: what is known about the individuals who become involved and finally the sources of socialization that lead to this involvement.

Research in this area (often carried out as much by journalists as academics) has attempted to answer three important questions. These are the what, who and why questions concerning children's involvement in political violence – that is what form of activity are they involved in, who are the children who become involved and why do they become involved?

The Stone Throwers

The vast majority of children who become involved in political violence, not surprisingly, take on relatively peripheral roles. Despite this, in certain societies where children and young people have become involved in political struggles, the media have tended to focus, almost exclusively, on their relative youthfulness.

That the media tend to focus so closely on the fact that young people and children are riot participants may be of special significance. Van Ginneken (1992) has pointed out for example, that the earliest crowd psychologist Taine, who wrote about the French revolution and served as a major source of inspiration for later nineteenth century writers on the subject, portrayed rioting crowds of that time as being made up largely of 'drunkards, criminals, women and children'. Further, he suggested that in a crowd people came to act 'like children' – who at that period were seen as representing more primitive forms of life.

A good example of this is the press coverage of rioting in Northern Ireland in the early 1970s. At this time street rioting was the most common form of political violence in Northern Ireland and children, according to contemporary reports, were very active, often being involved in confrontations with the security forces or, for example, in 'burning people out of their homes' (Fields, 1973). Indeed according to Fields the skill of these children became legendary with 'many of them . . . so expert in pitching rocks over vast distances with great accuracy as to surpass adult athletes'.

However, to put the role of children as rioters into perspective it is important to remember that only a relatively small proportion of the people of any age ever took part in the riots in Northern Ireland. For example, one study reported (Mercer and Bunting, 1980) that among a group of students, those who admitted to any 'contact' with rioting were less than 15 per cent of the total sample. Secondly, although young children were indeed involved, the majority of rioters in Northern Ireland tended to be in the 15–24 age group.

This is virtually the same age range as rioters in the racial disturbances which in the late 1960s shook major cities in the United States according to information contained in the Report of the National Advisory Commission on Civil Disorder (1968). This was a detailed report based on more that 1,200 interviews with eye witnesses, plus surveys of probability samples from riot areas in two major cities, and arrest records from 22 cities where rioting had occurred. The report again emphasizes the point that only a minority of people in riot areas ever become actual riot participants. For example, the National Commission estimated that only some 11 per cent of the 15 year-old plus population in areas where riots took place actually participated in the rioting. The remainder were either bystanders (25 per cent), or had nothing to do with the riots (48 per cent) while a further 16 per cent claimed to be 'counter-rioters'. This investigation was also able to quash the stereotype of the typical rioter as a person from the lowest levels of society. For example, the report recorded that the typical rioter, compared with other black people in the area (most rioters were black), tended to be somewhat better educated, better informed about politics, no more likely to come from a broken home and to be no poorer than his or her peers.

In more recent times two societies (South Africa and Palestine) where children and young people have been actively involved in political violence have grabbed the media headlines. Both these cases are of particular interest because they appear to contradict the impression, outlined above, that children's involvement in political violence is a peripheral one. In both these societies children and young people have been at the forefront, leaders rather than followers, in their particular political struggle.

In Palestine rioting and stone throwing brought the local children to the attention of the world's media. However, far from being a childish behaviour, according to Kuttab (1988) stone throwing amongst children in Palestine has been elevated to a military art with specific roles assigned to children of different ages. Those aged 7–10 years are given the job of rolling tyres into the middle of the road. These tyres are then set alight in order to disrupt traffic and attract Israeli soldiers.

The next youngest age group (11–14 years) use slingshots to attack passing cars. These two groups are used to prepare the ground for what Kuttab (1988) describes as the 'veteran stone throwers'. These young people use large rocks and inflict the worst damage on passing traffic and hence 'they are the most sought after by the Israelis'. This command structure is coordinated by older youths who from the vantage points they occupy determine which cars to attack for example, or when to retreat when the soldiers advance. Evidence of young people's prominent role in the 'Intifada' in Palestine comes from the fact 'the vast majority of deaths, injuries and cases of imprisonment occur among the younger generation' (Darweish, 1989).

The 'Young Lions' of South Africa became involved in political violence mainly through a protest movement which began in 1976 when security forces officially shot dead 25 (unofficially 100) young people who had gathered in Soweto to protest peacefully against educational changes (Liddell et al., 1993). Since then the movement has gathered strength and has been widened to become a more general mass democratic movement. For township children in South Africa the world, as a result, became a remarkably violent one 'made up of tear-gas, bullets, whippings, detentions and death on the streets' (Chikane, 1986). Evidence that children have been in the forefront of this campaign comes from the stark statistics that in the period between 1984 and 1986 alone some 300 children were killed by the police, 1,000 wounded, 11,000 detained without trial, 18,000 arrested on charges related to protest and 173,000 held in police cells (Simpson, 1993). From this mass youth movement a new generation of militants emerged. These young people became the political activists who spearheaded the political struggle in their country. They became involved in political leadership at a local level – for example, acting as marshals at mass funerals, creating street committees, even attending to civic matters and taking over local legal and administrative functions (Silove and Schweiter, 1993).

Despite concrete evidence for children and young people's active involvement in politics, understanding why young people, especially young children, take part in riots and demonstrations has proved to be rather more difficult. This question involves an issue that looms large over any discussion of children and young people's involvement in political violence – do children and young people adopt their own political perspective or one which others have prepared for them? Unfortunately, as Cook (1989) has noted, very few empirical studies have addressed this issue. Stewart (1977), an Irish historian has suggested that perhaps the latter is more likely. He has observed that when political violence broke out in the early 1970s the people of Northern Ireland

> turned instinctively to the only source of wisdom applicable to such circumstances – the inherited folk-memory of what had been done in the past, both good and bad. This atavism explains the emergence of patterns of behaviour which seemed to have little relevance to life in Northern Ireland between 1921 and 1969, but which were familiar to the historian. (Stewart, 1977, p. 185)

Others (e.g. Garbarino et al., 1991b) have speculated that children and young people may take part in political violence for the simple reason that they appreciate the thrill that comes with moderate danger and seek it out. Fraser (1974) suggests that this may account for the involvement of older children in the rioting in Belfast. Pre-adolescent children, he claims, became involved because, at this age, with their under-developed death concept, they were not psychologically capable of weighing up, in realistic terms, all the possible consequences of their actions.

One obvious factor about rioting and demonstrating is that they are also fundamentally collective actions. This may be the key to young people's political motivation. Whether one thinks about, at one extreme, the adolescents in France who joined the Maquis (the French underground army) because it had 'all the attractions of a great adventure', of belonging to a secret society, of engaging young boys through their love of adventure and play and above all their team spirit (International Child Welfare Review, 1947), or of the gang-related activities of boys in Belfast in the 1970s (Fraser, 1974) or the children in Palestine described by Punamaki (1987), the micro-social climate is probably the main factor in determining the sort of political response that children make.

Kuttab (1988) suggests that these children often begin their political careers by modelling the behaviour of and adopting the political ideology of their older brothers, favourite cousin or close school friend. However, determining the role of adults in shaping the political behaviour of young children is difficult. Fraser (1974) observed that in Belfast, in the early 1970s, adults tended to approve, at least tacitly, of the gangs formed by young people and indeed looked on them as a 'first line of area defence'. The role of adult males in organizing the Intifada in Palestine has been somewhat more overt (Usher, 1991). The role of parents is more enigmatic in these circumstances. Kuttab (1988) suggests that parents in Palestine could not stop their children even if they wanted to but that these parents in general supported their children's inolvement in political violence and indeed probably took a pride in it. Punamaki (1987) has also commented on the fact that Palestinian parents appear to admire their children's fearlessness although she hypothesizes that in doing so, parents may actually be denying their own feelings of anxiety and fear and in turn making it difficult for their children to use 'fear and horror as a ventilation of feelings'.

In South Africa, where children have been very involved in the political struggle, and at the local level at least as leaders, the relationship with parents appears to have been somewhat more fraught. Here, involvement with political violence apparently often placed a strain on families with children torn between loyalty to their radical political movement and their more conservative parents (Gibson, 1991). The outcome in such situations, she observes, meant that children, 'confronted with their parent's impotence in the face of danger, often experienced a disillusionment which fed into the process of separating from the family at adolescence'. On the other hand, in some families, involvement in political violence could lead to the creation of a form of 'political unity' (Gibson, 1991). This happened where, as a result of the threat to their children, previously conservative parents were 'drawn into sharing their children's more progressive beliefs'. The outcome was that the family was then united against a common (external) enemy. Burman (1986) suggests that what has happened in South Africa illustrates Piaget's idea that children do not simply absorb the values of their society but rather that they reinvent these values and in doing so, over time, alter society's understanding and consciousness. Children in South Africa, therefore, because of their involvement in political violence can be said to have altered the patterns and behaviour of the older generation in a remarkable way.

Ethnic pride may also be an important motivating factor. For example, among Palestinian young people according to Kuttab (1988) 'to throw a stone is to be one of the guys'. The National Advisory Commission on Civil Disorders also noted that a typical rioter in the US in the 1960s had strong feelings of racial pride if not racial superiority. Such people were, for example, more likely to want to be referred to as 'black' rather than 'negro' or 'coloured' and were more likely to believe that black people should study African history and languages. The report, however, also goes on to point out that whether this racial pride antedated the riots or whether it was itself caused by the riots is almost impossible to determine from the data available. If anything, however, the report comes down on the side of racial pride as cause rather than effect.

Mercer and Bunting (1980) in their study of riot participants in Northern Ireland suggest that, in this context, cause and effect may be meaningless terms. Instead, they hypothesized that young people who actively participate in political violence are caught up in a feedback loop. This would mean that the answer to the puzzle posed by the National Advisory Commission report is that racial pride is both a cause *and* an effect of political-protest participation.

The Paramilitaries

Activities such as stone throwing or taking part in mass protest actions require vast numbers of relatively young children. However, active involvement in political violence appears to tail off as children get older and in many societies overt action gives way to more clandestine activities often involving highly organized guerrilla movements. In large part, this is due to the nature of such organizations which do not require large numbers of participants but rather depend on relatively small, highly trained and dedicated volunteers. Strictly speaking therefore, guerrilla movements tend not involve children but rather are probably best thought of as 'youth movements' with most of their younger members in their teens (Waldmann, 1986). However, the members of these movements are of interest here because many observers believe that there is a natural progression from 'throwing stones and sticks to petrol bombs and gelignite' and from 'street gangs . . . to the IRA [Irish Republican Army] itself' (Fraser, 1974).

In many ways the young people who become involved in organized political violence, and who join paramilitary movements such as the IRA or the Basque ETA (Euzkadi ta Askatasuna), are among the most interesting of political activists. However, in comparison to the younger children – the stone throwers noted above – their older brothers and sisters have received relatively little attention from either the media or academics. This despite the fact that such young people make up a significant percentage of both liberation and national groups (Boothby, 1990, p. 31).

One reason for this lack of information is that paramilitary groups are usually clandestine organizations and therefore difficult to investigate. In particular the only members of paramilitary organizations available to researchers for interview are normally those who have either been caught and imprisoned and/or reformed – hardly a random selection of the membership of the organizations they once belonged to. Nevertheless, given the paucity of information in this area, although research on members of paramilitary organizations is difficult, it is also valuable. For this reason, according to Reich (1990), even when direct interaction with members of such organizations is not possible, attention should be paid to the words the terrorists use, their memoirs, their pronouncements, their rationales. Of course as Reich notes, these pronouncements may be self-serving. Despite this, he suggests they may still be revealing.

A further problem is that not only are members of these organizations difficult to access but also the whole phenomenon in which they are involved is a specially complex one. In particular, it could be claimed that each paramilitary group is unique and has therefore to be studied in the context of its own national culture and history (Post, 1990). Post has tried to simplify the situation to some extent by making the useful distinction between groups composed of anarchic/ideologues and those who are best described as nationalist/separatists. The dynamics of these two groups, he argues, are quite different because while both are against the existing political regime, in the former group this stance contrasts with that of their parents, while in the latter it does not. This means that only in the nationalist/separatist groups are young people able to maintain a relationship with their parents.

Terrorist Types

Notwithstanding the obvious difficulties involved, attempts have been made to understand the type of young person who becomes involved in political violence at this level. No doubt because of these difficulties noted earlier the literature contains only a limited amount of empirical research although it abounds with hypotheses. Perhaps the most frequently used explanation for this behaviour is that paramilitary groups attract those who are psychopaths. This, however, is a hypothesis which most academic observers in the area reject. Taylor (1988) for example notes that while it is possible to find some examples of paramilitaries who could clearly be said to be mentally ill the use of the label 'psychopath' is generally designed to make society feel better. It does little to promote the understanding of terrorism in general.

Hard evidence that young people involved in political violence are not so different from those who are not involved comes from a series of studies in Northern Ireland. Elliott and Lockhart (1980) were able to compare young people charged with 'political' (terrorist) offences with a control group of 'ordinary' juvenile delinquents. They concluded that both types of young offenders came from rather similar environments and had similar family backgrounds. The main differences that they noted were that the young men charged with the terrorist-type offences were likely to be more intelligent, have higher educational achievements and to be more socially outgoing. This study thus backed up the findings of two other studies involving young adults. The first of these (Boyle et al., 1976) had reported that people charged with terrorist offences were no different from those who had been involved with the law for 'ordinary' criminal offences, except that the ordinary criminals tended to be somewhat older. The second study (Lyons and Harbinson, 1986), was based on an examination of the case records of people in Northern Ireland who had been charged with murder over the period 1974–84. This concluded that 'political murderers' were generally more stable and came from stable family backgrounds in comparison to those who committed similar offences for non-political reasons. As Harris (1989, p. 88) has noted therefore, one of the frightening paradoxes of Northern Ireland is that it can be the 'well socialized and often dutiful young people of Belfast who have been responsible for much of the violence'.

Of course, none of these studies compared those who were members of paramilitary groups with the general population. It therefore may be true, as many authors have suggested, that because terrorists reside at the fringes of society, they therefore may attract proportionately more persons with mental illnesses (Reich, 1990). As a result paramilitary organizations may be made up of more mentally ill individuals than the general population. However, it is clear, as Reich concludes, that even if this is true the proportion is not strikingly high and that terrorists do not in general suffer from mental illnesses. Therefore, as Heskin (1980b) has noted it may be that psychopathic individuals in particular are attracted to conflict-oriented groups in order 'to indulge themselves with impunity'. This he notes, in the short term, may be useful to paramilitary organizations. However, in the long-term the 'egocentricity and unreliability' of such individuals, Heskin claims, would make them a 'dangerous liability' to any paramilitary group.

Other researchers have attempted to categorize members of paramiliatry organizations using a range of socio-demographic variables. The problem is, as Crenshaw (1990) has noted, that even if it were possible to say that most young people who become involved in paramilitary activities come from a particular social category, one would still be left with the fact that the majority of people from that category, in the population at large, almost certainly do not participate in terrorism. How then is it possible to explain the behaviour of the few that do?

In an attempt to solve this problem researchers have turned to more dynamic psychological explanations for terrorist behaviour. The results of this search have also tended to be disappointing. The overall conclusion appears to be that there is no particular terrorist type. Post (1990), however, maintains that although a wide range of personalities is attracted to terrorism, it is likely that people with particular personality traits are drawn disproportionately to terrorist 'careers'. In particular, Post has hypothesized that members of paramilitary groups tend to have one or all of the following personality traits – action oriented, aggressive and/or sensation seekers. Punamaki (1987), as a result of her observations of young people in the Middle East came to somewhat similar conclusions. However, she has added the important proviso that while aggressive children may go on to be freedom fighters, what determines that their aggressive response develops in this way is the social and political climate prevailing in their particular society during a crucial stage in their development. What she is referring to here is what Taylor (1988) has also referred to as the 'critical element' that emerges from the case histories of terrorists – the provision of the opportunity to join a terrorist group.

Much has also been made of the suggestion in the research literature (Merkle, 1986) that young people's involvement in political violence at this level may be as a result of a failure of the early bonding process. Conclusions of this kind tend to have been based on studies involving West German terrorists in the 1980s. Here, it was often reported that there was a high incidence of fragmented families. Some 25 per cent of those interviewed, for example, had lost one or both parents by the age of 14. Also, severe family conflict, especially with parents, was often reported, and the conclusion was drawn that many of these young people tended to be 'advancement oriented and failure prone'. As a result of evidence such as this, Post (1990, p. 25) has argued that becoming involved in political violence is not a matter of intentional choice rather:

> that political terrorists are driven to commit acts of violence as a consequence of psychological forces and that their special psycho-logic is constricted to rationalize acts they are psychologically compelled to commit.

What he means by this, apparently, is that the terrorists are driven to destroy the establishment because of their own need to search for identity. Striking out against the establishment is an attempt to 'destroy the enemy within'. Post has therefore called particular attention to the psychological processes of 'externalizing' and 'splitting'. These he claims are psychological mechanisms that are found in individuals with narcissistic and borderline personality disturbances. And while he does not suggest that all young people involved in paramilitary violence exhibit such borderline personality disorders he does claim that these mechanisms are found with 'extremely high frequency in the population of terrorists'. In particular, he makes much of the process of 'splitting' in which an individual splits out and projects out onto others all the hated and devalued weaknesses within. Such individuals, Post maintains, tend to look outward for the source of difficulties in their lives and need an outside enemy to blame. Further, such young people he suggests find the 'polarizing absolutist rhetoric' of terrorism very attractive because it is psychologically satisfying to believe that 'they' (the rest of society) are the cause of all that has gone wrong in their own personal lives.

Many young people who have become involved in paramilitary political violence, as well as many political scientists, would abhor such a psychological analysis. However, as Crenshaw (1990) has noted, applying a psychological analysis to terrorism is not meant to be a dismissal of terrorism as an irrational act. Nor is it meant to be seen as an insistence that emotions dominate over-rational political behaviour. Instead, she believes that a psychological approach need not deny that political commitment or that terrorist calculations can be logical. However, she does point out that there are many important research questions that need to be answered in this area. In particular, the question of whether terrorists are different from non-terrorists because of personality, socialization or opportunity must be addressed. Other questions needing further research are how are young people recruited into paramilitary organizations and is the conversion sudden or gradual? And what role does personal disappointment within non-violent politics play? In particular do political beliefs proceed or result from participation in terrorism and if moral inhibitions exist among young people involved in political violence at this level how are they overcome?

Motivations

It is obvious that terrorism is a complex problem and that it attracts a wide range of individuals to its ranks, but individuals who are difficult to classify in either sociodemographic or psychological terms. At the same time, there seems to be little concrete evidence that terrorism is structurally produced (Crenshaw, 1990). In other words, theories that suggest that environmental factors such as social class or economics hold the exclusive key are equally to be found wanting. Rather than looking for types of individuals who become involved in this sort of political violence it may make more sense to try to determine what motivates individuals to behave in this way. Again, it is clear that it is difficult to generalize about the motivations for individuals; nor is any one theory from any one academic discipline going to provide all the answers.

One of the obvious places to look for an answer in order to try to understand just what young people might get out of joining a paramilitary organization is to examine the rewards involved. To begin with there may be material rewards. For those who joined the Nazi movement in occupied Europe, for example, this could mean more money, more food, a car to drive and the lifting of the threat of deportation to Germany (International Child Welfare Review, 1947). Even today, being in an apparently lowly paramilitary organization can bring material rewards. Assal and Farrel (1992) record an exchange with a young Lebanese girl who explained that while her high-school teacher earned $160 per month and had to stand in line for bread, her brother, a militia member, earned $230 and could walk to the front of any food line.

In addition, many observers agree that there is likely to be a certain amount of prestige associated with such membership, perhaps even glamour (Heskin, 1980b). This may be especially important for young people. As Rosenblatt (1983, p. 101) has noted, becoming involved in war allows 'boys to look like men'. Part of the prestige undoubtedly comes from the sense of power that membership in a paramilitary organization can confer. In particular, for young people there is the possibility of wielding power over adults, for example teachers and even parents. In Nazi society children could inform and indeed were encouraged to inform on erring parents or teachers (McArdle, 1949). Likewise, in Soviet Russia, where children could betray their parents either wittingly or unwittingly, fear of children was not unknown (Geiger, 1968). In this way, in certain societies the power structure in the family can be turned upside down. For example, in Zimbabwe (Reynolds, 1990) children became involved in the national struggle as messengers between villagers and the freedom fighters. This privileged position was, however, open to abuse as children could hold power over adults by threatening to denounce them to the paramilitaries. What is interesting is that Reynolds (1990, p. 8) notes that after the war such children 'were firmly placed back in the niche of childhood' once more at the bottom of the village pecking order.

As noted in chapter 3, war can be exciting for children. Added to this general excitement may be the thrill of belonging to a secret organization, perhaps handling weapons, attending clandestine meetings etc. Burton (1979), an English sociologist, who lived in the early 1970s in a part of West Belfast where the IRA was active, observed that boredom was a major problem for the young men of the district and that membership of the IRA was one way of relieving that boredom. Finally, there is of course 'the comfort of belonging to a community of the like-minded' (Crenshaw, 1990). Post (1990, p. 36) has summarized all of these factors as follows:

> Before joining the group, he was alone, not particularly successful. Now he is engaged in a life and death struggle with the establishment . . . He sees his leaders as internationally prominent media personalities. Within certain circles, he is lionized as a hero. He travels first class, and his family is provided for should his acts of heroism lead to his death as a martyr to the cause.

Some would claim that this paints too rosy a picture of life for a young person in paramilitary organization. They would argue that other explanations need to be sought in order to understand the behaviour of young people who are prepared to sacrifice a normal life, even life itself, for a political cause. If one rejects the idea that membership of a paramilitary group confers rewards, or at least if one rejects the idea that this is what initially leads young people to join such an organization, then an alternative explanation involves some form of political socialization.

Political Socialization

Political socialization received extensive attention from researchers in the 1960s and 1970s. Much of this work was devoted to deciding which of the various socialization agents such as the family, the schools, churches or the media were most responsible for shaping children's political views. At one time, the family was thought to be 'the most important factor' (Almond, 1960) and 'foremost among the agents of socialization into politics' (Hyman, 1959). Gradually, however, this view appeared to receive less and less empirical support. Today it could be said that the family is making something of a comeback. Current opinion suggests that the family can be an important source of political socialization but only under certain restricted conditions. In particular three conditions have been highlighted. These are that the parents share the same political views, that politics is important to both parents and that finally the child perceives that politics is important to his/her parents (Barner-Barry and Rosenwein, 1985).

One situation in which such conditions almost certainly apply is among families living in societies where nationalist/separatist groups exist. Here, the influence of history and family traditions often appears to be decisive in the process of socialization. For example, according to Taylor (1988), Gerry Adams the President of Sinn Fein (the political wing of the IRA in Ireland), illustrates the role of family commitment to revolutionary politics. Taylor records that Adam's father was shot and wounded in the 1940s and that he had two uncles who were leading activists in the IRA campaign at that time. Forty years later he himself was similarly involved while a brother was sentenced for IRA activities. Some insight into this process comes in an interview with a former IRA volunteer recorded by Coogan (1987, p. 284). This man reported that he joined the IRA while he was 16 and still at school. 'It was the result of the environment in which I grew up. My father had been killed fighting in 1922 . . . I think my decision to join the IRA was inevitable because with my upbringing and background it would have been shirking a duty not to do so.'

This is not of course to suggest that parents necessarily give direct political instruction to their children. Instead, what probably happens is that children overhear parental conversations or that they informally learn of their parents' political views. Also, parents are required to answer questions about politics 'just as they are asked to answer a thousand and one other questions as children grow up' (Greenstein, 1969).

Clark (1986), as a result of his study of members of the ETA in the Basque region of Spain, concluded that the family can play an important role in the making of a guerrilla fighter. He notes that 'it may be something of an exaggeration to say that the making of an etarra begins in the cradle, but almost certainly it begins quite soon thereafter'. Despite this he found that only in the lives of a very few of the young men he interviewed did the families play a direct role. However, parents do play an indirect role and evidence for this process can be found in the course of interviews recorded in Northern Ireland by the journalist Peter Taylor. These are reproduced in his excellent book *Families at War*. In particular his interview with a mother in Belfast, three of whose four sons had been killed while on active service with the IRA, is revealing. Despite all this the mother denied that she had in any way directly influenced her children. However, she did recount that while she had not fed them on 'rabble-rousing Republicanism' she had 'encouraged their sense of Irishness' and through bedtime stories made sure that they always understood Irish history. What comes out from this and other interviews in Taylor's book is that direct indoctrination may be the exception rather than the rule even in politically-committed families. In this context, of course, it is important to remember that political feelings form well before the child begins to understand anything about the political issues involved (Greenstein, 1965).

Socialization in the family may also occur in much more subtle ways. So subtle that often it is difficult if not impossible to observe or study. For example, in South Africa, children, in politically-active families, are sometimes named after political leaders in the ANC (African National Congress) (Dawes, 1990). As Dawes notes, this way of naming the child is a politically symbolic act and may well be instrumental in constructing the child's political views from birth. In a similar vein in Israel, among members of the Israeli Defence Force, there is a tradition of naming children after fallen comrades – a practice that no doubt exists in other parts of the world. Yet another example is in Northern Ireland where parents may be taking steps to influence their children's attitudes even before the child is born by selecting a particular first name which signals to others whether that child is a Catholic or a Protestant (Cairns, 1992). In Northern Ireland and in other societies this naming may have particular significance. In common with many other societies children in Ireland are often named 'after' relatives or family friends. If the child's namesake is an a revered adult who is or has been actively involved in a paramilitary organization this may create a powerful role mode. This is of course speculation. However, as selective naming of children is one example of the more subtle forms of socialization that can actually be observed, it deserves further study.

Obviously, it would be wrong to suggest that families are the only socialization agents at work in societies where children become involved in political violence. Another important institution is the school. Once again the evidence is largely anecdotal. What it suggests is that at the very least schools can play a role in increasing young people's susceptibility to the attractions of terrorism (Crenshaw, 1990). Again, the interviews in Taylor's (1989) book provide some insight into this process. In particular, he outlines a case where the education system, rather than the family, appears to have been the primary socializing factor in stimulating a young boy to dedicate himself to a paramilitary cause.

This comes in an interview with a former IRA activist whose family had, while aspiring to the reunification of Ireland, always stayed aloof from the use of violence to this end. In this middle class home education had been the main focus of family life rather than politics. This young man was at elementary school in the 1960s. This, it should be remembered, was a decade or so before the current unrest in Northern Ireland erupted; it was a time, as Taylor recalls, when most boys of that age were obsessed with Manchester United or the Beatles. However, what this little Irish boy was most interested in at that time was reading about the patriots and founding fathers of the Irish nation.

According to Taylor, at a much later date, under the floorboards in his home, a letter was found that he had hidden when he was aged about 10 or 11 years of age. In this letter, written as Taylor notes, as another boy might have written to Santa Claus, the boy asked that he might be given the possibility of joining the IRA and of becoming a hero and a martyr and of dying for Ireland. According to the informant himself and his brother, the source of these romantic dreams were the 'excessively nationalistic tones' of the history books used in the elementary school which he attended. This story, along with the way in which Hitler used the educational system to capture the 'hearts and minds' of young people in the 1930s, plus the account of life in post-war Russia serve as a useful reminder, that 'when the school is pitted against the family, the latter is the looser' (Geiger, 1968, p. 309).

In this context the teaching of history in particular appears to be a key element. For example, Kuttab (1988) reports that children in Palestine may be taught the name of the village that their family came from despite the fact that the village may actually have been destroyed by the Israelis some 40 years ago. Of course, such teaching may not necessarily be undertaken on a formal basis. In both South Africa and Palestine that disruption in the official school system allowed the development of 'people's education' which provided an opportunity to politicize young people and to emphasize the liberation struggle (Adam, 1990). Kuttab (1988) also reports that children in Palestine could be socialized into politics by such things as the songs sung on important occasions, for example, at weddings. Indeed, it may be that the combination of history and music plays a special role. Searching for a political ideology as a student in the 1960s at university in Belfast, and disillusioned with the established student political clubs, Bernadette Devlin (1969) soon became a leading figure in the civil-rights movement in Northern Ireland. It is reported in her autobiography that she found 'more real politics in the Folk Music Society' than in any of the political parties at that time.

Misleadingly, the early literature tended to give the impression that political socialization consists of a once and for all, never to be repeated, dose of politics in early life. Today, it is understood that political socialization can take place at any time during a person's life-span, although a crucial time may be late adolescence and early adulthood. One important setting in which such activities may occur is when young people are incarcerated for their political activities. For example, young political detainees in South Africa have reported that their political resolve was actually strengthened by imprisonment because their prison cells often became the location for intensive political education (Dawes, 1990). In a similar vein it has often been said that the prison system in Northern Ireland quickly became the 'IRA's university of terrorism', with endless hours during which prisoners read and discussed revolutionary socialism and planned for the years ahead (Taylor, 1989).

Finally, in today's world of satellite dishes and video recorders one cannot rule out a possible role for the media in political socialization. One suggestion is that the media may play a role because they ensure that people no longer 'consider their fate in isolation from other world events' (Adam, 1990). In particular Adam suggests that dominated people in one part of the world may be inspired by events that they see happening in another part of the world. Certainly, many observers have speculated that it was no coincidence that the conflict in Northern Ireland took a new form with street demonstrations and riots just at the time (1967–8) when similar events were happening in Italy, France and Czechoslovakia (Arthur, 1974).

A less obvious way that young people can become involved in political activity is either by being themselves the victims of violence or by witnessing violent behaviours and attitudes that are unpunished or positively sanctioned (McKendrick and Hoffmann, 1990). The literature on children and political violence is replete with observations which suggest that some form of victimization may play a major role in channelling children and young people towards taking violent political action. Before discussing exactly how this might happen it is important to note that for the majority of children such an experience probably leads to passive acceptance of violence. Indeed, in some cases such an experience can lead to insecurity, perhaps to depression and the 'classic slave mentality', because anger is turned inwards (Knutson, 1981). In other cases children's feelings of hate and aggression may be dealt with by identifying with the aggressor. This, according to Ronstrom (1989) is what sometimes happened in Central America, in particular with boys whose fathers had been killed by the army.

In other circumstances however, it is claimed that experiences of political repression are more likely to lead to the formation of political consciousness (Dawes, 1990). For example, children who see their parents humiliated in Palestine according to Usher (1991), react with aggression, indeed with a kind of fearless defiance, against the forces of occupation, while in Zimbabwe 'again and again' the impetus for boy soldiers to leave home and fight was 'the brutality of the Rhodesian Security Forces' (Reynolds, 1990, p. 5). Similarly, in South Africa it has been suggested that young people, because of their experiences of police harassment and violence, 'came to the conclusion that there was only one option open to them and that was to take up arms' (Chikane, 1986, p. 334).

The literature on Northern Ireland also contains examples of victimization as an energizing experience. Knutson (1981) conducted interviews with members of the IRA in the late 1970s. In one, the respondent recalls how he grew up in an integrated area of Belfast with little or no interest in politics. All of this changed one day, when, in his early teens, his house was attacked and burned to the ground. Interviewed in his late twenties, what he recalled of this was the sheer terror, the fear that it would happen again and the growing realization that 'my best means of defence was to attack' (Knutson, 1981, p. 43). This interview, conducted by Knutson, also fits in with press reports concerning the hunger strikers of 1981, all of whom, according to reports (*Irish Times*, May, 13, 1981) had been through similar experiences, ranging from being shot in the foot by the British Army at age twelve (Patsy O'Hara) to being beaten up at a security forces checkpoint at the age of seventeen (Francis Hughes).

Victimization does not have to be personally experienced in order for it to lead to politicization. Vicariously experienced victimization may also have this effect. In these cases some form of survivor guilt may play a role. For example, Ayalon (1983) notes that in Israel he observed that victims who harbour the most anger and vengeance are often those who are saved unharmed. To illustrate this point, he relates the story of a young man who became involved in a terrorist situation as a hostage. By volunteering to take a message out of the building he was spared death. Later, as a soldier involved in military action in the Lebanon, he became known as someone who was 'carrying out a private war of revenge for his murdered mates'. In this way, according to Ayalon (1983), he succeeded in 'releasing an enormous personal pressure'.

A somewhat similar picture emerges from Taylor's (1989) interview with the mother of Mairead Farrell, the young Irish woman shot dead in disputed circumstances by British forces in Gibraltar in 1988. According to her mother the incident that determined that Mairead would 'have to make her contribution', and which subsequently led to her joining the IRA, was the blinding of the mother of a school friend by a rubber bullet fired by a British soldier (Taylor, 1989).

Boy Soldiers

It is of course important to remember that children have been part of state military organizations for centuries. The earliest record of children going to war is probably the children's crusade of 1212 when two armies of children from France and Germany joined with adult soldiers in a crusade to recapture the Holyland (Daly and Vaughan, 1988).

In today's world, children and young people in state-run military organizations may not hit the headlines in the same as those involved in rioting or in guerilla groups but nevertheless they still exist. For example in the Iraq/Iran war boys as young as 13 years were reportedly forced to join the Iranian army while those younger than this were encouraged to join. These children apparently were often used for tasks such as searching the battlefield for unexploded mines. According to one report (*Le Matin,* 11 December 1984) the Iranian government made a special point of recruiting children who had lost their fathers in the war. In special schools these children, as young as four years, were taught the basic precept that the state President was now their father and that it was their duty as men to go to war and to sacrifice themselves for their country.

Similar reports of the existence of boy soldiers have come from wars in Zimbabwe, Mozambique and Cambodia. In some of these places children were kidnapped and forced into military service. But this is not always the case. In societies such as the Lebanon, children were recruited and indoctrinated using programs that glorified violence. Learning by doing is also often an important part of the training, with children forced to carry out brutal acts towards civilians, or even colleague, as 'rites of passage' (Macksoud et al., 1993).

Learning to Kill

Whatever the initial stimulus for children and young people who become actively involved in politics, whether through a process of socialization, victimization or simply a desire for status or other rewards, a further question to be investigated is why do some of these activists not only become involved in politics but also become involved in violent politics?

Recruitment into a paramilitary organization usually takes time and in addition involves a degree of direct instruction. This, according to McCauley and Segal (1987) is an important point in understanding how 'normal and even idealistic' people can become 'terrorists'. Their point is that radical behaviour is something that is acquired gradually, something that progresses from the less to the more extreme.

Even the process of recruitment itself may take some time. Clark (1986) in his study of ETA members in Spain notes that even after initial recruitment the young person will almost certainly enter a 'novice' phase which will last for some weeks or months, perhaps even years. During this initial phase the organization may try out the new recruit in various ways. Usually this entails asking him/her to carry out relatively innocuous tasks such as delivering political pamphlets. Once this stage of initiation has been successfully passed the recruit may be asked to participate in operations that are more complex and therefore more dangerous. This might include, for example, gathering intelligence or delivering weapons. All of this of course means that it is difficult to say when new members actually cross the threshold and become fully fledged members of the organization.

One important consequence of becoming involved in even relatively innocuous activities is that the young person almost certainly grows in his or her commitment to the group and its ideals. This is because this period involves a period of learning by doing, during which core values are developed. Therefore as Staub (1989, p. 89) points out:

> Even if initially there is some external pressure, it often becomes difficult to experience regular participation in an activity as

> alien. People begin to see their engagement in the activity as part of themselves.

During this period direct training may also be given. Bandura (1990) notes that this may include extensive training in moral disengagement as well as training in actual military prowess. In many cases, the processes involved in training for moral disengagement may involve using euphemisms to neutralize antisocial acts, the diffusion of responsibility, detaching oneself from the consequences of violent action and dehumanizing the victim (Bandura, 1990). Deutch (1990) has proposed that the way in which this dehumanizing process may take place is by means of what he calls 'moral splitting'. This, he claims, allows definite boundaries to develop between 'us' and 'them'. When this has been achieved it becomes easier for 'us' to exclude 'them' from the moral community and to begin to regard 'them' as not entitled to moral and justice considerations. The final outcome of this process is that it 'allows one to consider oneself as a moral person even while one engages in what would normally be considered depraved actions' (Deutch, 1990, p. 24).

Perhaps one of the best known recent incidents in which moral splitting hit the headlines is the Mai Lai massacre. According to Kohlberg (1984, p. 571), one of the notable facts to emerge from interviews with soldiers involved in this incident was that they justified their action because they saw what they did as 'essentially a group action taken on the basis of group norms'. This, of course, highlights the collective nature of this event and indeed of all politically-motivated violence and in turn emphasises the role of social identity as a key variable (see chapter 1 for more details).

Moral splitting is not always successful however, and when it fails, an opportunity is provided to learn more about the processes involved. Linn (1989) has attempted to do this by interviewing members of the Israeli Defence Forces who refused to take part in certain military actions – particularly in the occupied territories (Palestine). She claims that two types of morality are involved – a morality of obligation/duty and also a morality of belonging/loyalty. The latter she suggests is an aspect of morality that has been neglected in the psychological literature on moral development and again could be thought of as a form of morality linked to social identity (see chapter 3 on moral development and chapter 6).

Soldiers who refuse orders, such as those noted above, appear to be the exception. More often than not, the outcome of military training is the development of the capacity to kill which 'usually evolves through a process in which recruits may not fully recognize the transformations they are undergoing' (Bandura, 1990, p. 185). This process of gradual indoctrination into an organization, which is designed ultimately to produce children who kill is, as noted above, not confined to extra-state organizations.

The question of what happens in the long term to children socialized into violence for political ends has received little if any empirical attention. However, what information there is suggests that there is only limited support for the fear that when children are taught to engage in violence for political ends it will promote a different understanding of the morality of violent action.

In other words, the evidence suggests that children who become political activists will confine their violent behaviour within the context of the political struggle (Dawes, 1990). That is, according to Dawes's observations in South Africa, endorsement of violence in a political context is not necessarily an endorsement of violence per se. This is exactly what experience in Northern Ireland appears to be suggesting (see chapter 3). Children and young people appear able to maintain the distinction between violence for a just cause and violence which is seen to be unjust (Gibson, 1989).

There is, however, according to Dawes (1992), one situation in which political violence may generalize to other areas of life. This is where a young person has attained a particular reputation for aggressiveness in the political sphere and around this type of behaviour has developed a unique identity. In circumstances such as these, according to Dawes, there is the possibility that violence can become a central element in the young person's identity and could therefore be maintained after the initial political motives for such behaviour are no longer applicable.

Summary

Most of the literature concerned with children and political violence portrays children as the passive victims of political violence. However, children are not always *passive* victims, there is evidence that they can be politically active.

This raises three basic questions – in what way are children involved, who are these children (that is how are they different from their peers), and what motivates them to become politically active?

Children's involvement falls into two main categories. By far the largest of these consists of younger children who are involved at the periphery, often in such overt political activities as rioting or demonstrating. Older children are more likely to be involved in clandestine activities as members of a terrorist organization.

The larger group, the 'stone throwers', are perhaps better known because of media interest in them. Not only are these children in most societies a minority of all children but they are probably older than the media likes to suggest. In some societies, however, for example in South Africa and Palestine this form of activity may involve a majority of young people and their role can become more central to the political struggle.

A variety of hypotheses have been entertained as to why children become involved in this form of street politics. These include the thrill of danger, extension of gang-related activities common at this age or the possibility that they are modelling themselves on adult behaviour. A more worrying suggestion is that the role of adult involvement is more overt – the Godfather hypothesis.

This raises the question of the relationship of these children with their families: do families approve, encourage, admire, or do they disapprove? In terms of hard evidence we know very little about these or other questions. Basically we know that children are involved but we don't know why.

Membership of paramilitary groups or guerrilla armies probably involves smaller numbers of children and young people who, as noted above, are often slightly older than their stone-throwing brother and sister. In this area it may be important to recognize two types of groups, anarchic/ideologues and nationalist/separatists. Probably more children and young people join the latter.

It is clear that it is not possible to fit these young people into any particular socio-demographic or psychological categories. In particular there is little evidence to support the common claim that guerrilla organizations attract a disproportionate number of psychopathic individuals.

Nor is it likely that there is a particular 'terrorist type' – even with wide criteria such action-oriented, aggressive, and sensation-seeking. Rewards may play a role such as prestige, glamour, excitement and even material rewards. It is not clear, however, if these are the reasons people join in the first place; or are these factors which sustain membership?

Rather than suggesting that individuals are motivated to become political activists because of certain psychological characteristics or because of the lure of rewards, it is hypothesized that children are socialized into this role in subtle ways, particularly via the indirect impact of institutions such as the family. Also there is the possibility that schools may influence children's political ideas in certain societies, especially through the teaching of history. Of course, not all history is taught in schools and in more recent times media coverage of other political struggles has also been implicated in this socialization process as paradoxically have prisons. There is also some intriguing qualitative evidence that being a victim or witnessing another become one may play a role in stimulating young people to become politically involved.

Finally, the UN convention notwithstanding, it must be remembered that there are still many state-run armies around the world that include children in their ranks.

Whichever organization a child or young person becomes a member of he or she may be taught to kill. It appears that in many clandestine organizations the recruitment period is used as a selection phase and/or as an indoctrination phase to prepare for this event. Low-level activities are involved to begin with then these gradually escalate to allow moral disengagement to take place.

As conflicts come to an end the fear is often expressed that members of groups trained to kill or maim young people will not be able to be resocialized. Anecdotal evidence suggests that this is not necessarily true. One possible explanation, which is yet to be tested empirically, is that a key element in membership of paramilitary groups may be the development of a morality of loyalty which in turn is related to the development of a relevant situated social identity.

This is obviously a very difficult to area in which to get hard evidence. The existing evidence therefore comes from atypical group members; it is largely anecdotal and has mostly been gathered by journalists rather than social scientists. It could be argued, however, that scholars could make more use of these as primary sources. Probably the only thing we can claim to have any firm evidence on is that children and young people who join nationalist/separatist guerrilla movements are not psychopaths and come from no particular social strata of society. Other hypotheses, including ideas of 'terrorist personality types' or psychodynamic explanations, will always be very hard to substantiate.

5 Children and Peace

As the rest of this book has shown, researchers have been chronicling the negative impact that political violence can have on children for almost 100 years. It could, however, be argued that while much has been written eloquently testifying to the desperate need to protect children from this experience, the academic community has put comparatively little effort into thinking about how that protection could be provided.

In other words, there has been little research aimed at bringing political violence to an end. This chapter will therefore be very different from the preceding chapters and indeed from the many chapters that have been written on the topic of children and political violence: it will consider how psychology can contribute to bringing political violence to an end.

Before looking at the more technical aspects of this question the chapter will begin by considering if children once exposed to political violence can contemplate not simply a future without political violence, but any kind of a future at all.

Visions of the Future

Modern cognitive and developmental psychologists have found the idea of schema or representation a useful one. Put simply, a schema is a cognitive structure that is constructed by the individual in order to organize previously acquired information and to influence memory. In a similar way social psychologists have come to speak of 'social representations' that are consensual understandings which emerge from informal discussion and transform the unfamiliar into the familiar by providing a framework of knowledge which helps to satisfy our need to understand the world (Hogg and Abrams, 1988).

Majhoub et al. (1989) are convinced that political violence is not simply an external reality for children but also becomes part of the child's representations of the world. In particular, Majhoub et al. (1989) take the view that the experience of political violence not only conditions the shaping of the past and the present for children but also of the future. Given the terrifying experiences that some children may be subjected to as a result of political violence, it is perhaps not surprising that these children may develop representations of themselves and the future which are very limited if not overtly pessimistic (Maksoud, Dyregrov and Raundalen, 1993).

For example, Assal and Farrel (1992) in the context of their work with children in the Lebanon, recorded that if there was one phrase that was repeated to them 'time and time again' it was the equivalent of 'I see no future ahead of us in the Lebanon'. Similarly, Roe (in press) in his work with child evacuees in the Philippines and Central America, noted a marked lack of 'futurity'. This phenomenon, which he refers to as 'atemporality', he suggests is characterized as a longing for a past without violence, little investment in the present, and a future that is perceived as uncertain.

One piece of empirical evidence which supports this hypothesis comes from the studies described earlier by Rautman and Brower (1945; 1951). These had been conducted in the same US city, with children of the same age and background at two time points: during the war and five years after it had ended. All the children were asked to write stories in response to TAT pictures. What these authors report is that during the war only 35 per cent of the children produced happy endings (25 per cent sad) and that these figures changed to 51 per cent and 15 per cent, respectively, in 1950. Rautman and Brower (1951) therefore concluded that compared with the elementary child of the war period the 1950 children were 'more optimistic in their outlook'.

One possible reason for a lack of optimism concerning the future during war-time is the discontinuity which can be created by political violence between children and their parents or perhaps even more importantly their grandparents. Among other things, this means that children may lack role models which are essential for the transmissions of attitudes and values which have been found useful in their particular culture in dealing with the world (Burman, 1986).

In contrast to this, other investigators have observed that children exposed to political violence have tended to write about the future in rather more positive and optimistic ways. In particular such children may stress the role of education as a way of improving their life chances (Raundalen et al., 1987). Ressler et al., (1988) have suggested that this is possible even for traumatized children who have lost their parents, because at least some of them manage to idealize and identify with parental and cultural values through memories of better times. This identification with the past is used, among other things, to encourage a view of a more hopeful future. Unfortunately, this may be an option that is open only to older children and adolescents who remember a time before the impact of political violence.

Such children, Ressler et al. (1988) suggest, 'have consciously connected their efforts to learn and achieve in the present to expectations and values bequeathed to them by their parents in the past' (p. 165). One of the main guiding notions of such children, therefore, becomes 'this is what my parents would expect of me'. A related factor is that young refugees often know that their parents made great personal and financial sacrifices to flee from their home countries (van der Veer, 1993). As noted earlier (chapter 2) internalization of parental norms from the past and thus the development of a positive future perspective is important not just in terms of normal personal development. It may also play an important role in the way children cope with the trauma to which they have been subjected (Mahjoub et al., 1989; van der Veer, 1993). (Given the fact that the age at which children are separated from their parents appears to be a key variable in the coping literature this deserves closer attention in work related to the development of a future perspective.)

While most of the research in this area is based on anecdotal evidence a more systematic empirical effort to examine young people's future orientation in relation to political violence is that undertaken by Danziger (1963a; 1963b). Set in the context of South Africa, the first study involved young African, Indian and White English speakers and White Afrikaans speakers, either in the last year of high school or the first year of university. All were asked to write a short essay on the history of South Africa projected into the future. The contents of the essays were then classified according to whether they adopted one of five approaches. The categories were:

(a) conservative – the absence of real change;
(b) technicist – where change is seen as essential material;
(c) catastrophic – where the present situation is seen as deteriorating;
(d) liberal – change seen as gradual and relatively smooth; and
(e) revolutionary – where the future is seen in terms of violent development.

What is interesting is that the different groups tended to see the future differently. The greatest proportion of Afrikaans-speaking young people envisaged either a conservative or a technicist future while the English-speaking whites were most likely to foresee a future that ended in catastrophy. Among the Indian respondents a liberal future was the most likely outcome while the African young people tended to see the future in terms of revolution.

An interesting attempt was made, on a much more limited basis, to use the same technique with a group of young people in Northern Ireland (McWhirter, 1983). Unfortunately the sample was extremely limited apparently consisting almost totally of middle-class, Protestant girls. Nevertheless, it is interesting to compare the results from these members of the dominant group in Northern Ireland with those obtained from the dominant group (white Afrikaans speakers) in South Africa. What the results indicated was that again the most commonly held view of the future was a conservative one. These two studies therefore seem to suggest that dominant groups are likely to be the last to see any change in the status quo. This in turn confirms Danzinger's (1963a) conclusion that an individual's orientation to the social future is a function of the manner in which he/she experiences the relationship between rulers and ruled. This hypothesis has been confirmed by recent research in South Africa undertaken in the context of the rapid change in political conditions there (Dawes and Finchilescu, 1993). This work, again asking children to write essays on the future of South Africa, found that both conservative and revolutionary futures were much less commonly envisaged than thirty years earlier. A slender majority of white adolescents (both Afrikaans and English-speaking) were now more apprehensive of the future, which they saw as 'catastrophic' (the next most common future was 'liberal'). The great majority of their black conterparts (African and Indian) now tended to see the futures as 'liberal' (a minority saw it as catastrophic). These differences were more clearly seen in the essays written by younger (12 year olds) than by the older (17 year olds) participants.

The authors claim that these ideas about the future were clearly linked to the feeling that the white group was loosing political power to the black majority. Overall it is encouraging to note, however, that a clear majority of these young South African people were apparently looking forward to a 'liberal' future.

In a related study Danziger (1963b) focused in on the 'personal' future by asking different young African high-school students in South Africa in three different years – 1950, 1956 and 1962 – to write an essay that was basically autobiographical. In this the students were asked to say something about their own expectations, plans and aspirations for the future. As Danziger points out, the period over which these essays were collected was a particularly interesting one in the history of South Africa covering the period from the first attempts to launch the apartheid programme to the first appearance of resistance in the form of political violence.

These essays were scored in various ways. For example, each essay was coded for the mention of personal plans and goals that were realistic, personal plans and goals that were on the level of phantasy and plans and goals that involved social issues. Over the period 1950–62 the number of young people mentioning realistic personal plans and goals decreased, whereas the number mentioning social issues tended to increase.

Danziger (1963b) also made an attempt to look for any change in individual time perspectives brought on by the apartheid campaign. What he reports is that in 1950, his African respondents tended to anchor their future plans in an objective temporal framework (much as white males did at that time). By 1962, however, many fewer African young people were adopting this perspective. This he suggests may be 'the result of a growing feeling of helplessness in the face of apparently official interference in the individual's personal life' (p. 36).

The essays were also used to determine the type of life goals and values that the young African writers espoused. Two main types of life goals were noted, one involving economic success the other community service (excluding direct political activity). The results revealed that at each of the three time periods when data were collected, rather more of the respondents saw their future in terms of community service. For example, the essay writers saw themselves in the future as teachers, nurses or doctors, that is in jobs which would enable them to 'help my people' or 'uplift the African masses'. In this respect the results of this study echo those of an earlier essay writing investigation that compared Swiss teenagers and Jewish refugees in Switzerland during World War II. This Swiss study found that the young Jewish people's essays revealed more concern with the future, and in particular 'a marked collective egosim' in which service to their own community was the highest ideal to which they aspired (McArdle, 1949, p. 249). (These results again serve to highlight the fact that exposure to political violence is essentially a collective experience and one that impacts more on social identity than it does on personal identity.)

Finally, in the South African study, there was a decline in the number of respondents mentioning either of these life goals over the period 1950–62 . Again Danziger (1963b) suggests that these results may be related to growing feelings of futility on the part of his young essay writers. For example he noted that the number of people mentioning political activity in the cause of African Nationalism increased from 7 per cent in 1950 to 42 per cent in 1956, although it then declined to 28 per cent in 1962. Of course one would not wish to make too much of Danziger's results – the numbers are rather small and his sample was by no means random or representative. Nevertheless, one is tempted to conclude that these results reveal the possibility of profound changes in the psychological future of young people who have been exposed to political violence.

Is Peace an Option?

While it is encouraging to note that children caught up in political violence do, in the main, still have long-term goals it could be argued that future plans about careers, marriage and so on are a luxury only for those young people who have managed to escape from the immediate surrounding of political violence. For those still involved in political violence on a day-to-day basis one might imagine the most pressing, perhaps the only concern for the future in the short-term is likely to be the possibility of peace. But is this true? Again there is a limited amount of empirical data plus much anecdotal evidence. Again the evidence is, on the face of it, contradictory.

One school of thought, which has been most clearly articulated by Punamaki (1987), believes that children who are growing up in a society which is based on 'hate' and 'the denial of human values' cannot be successfully socialized or indeed resocialized into 'a peace-loving citizen'. Punamaki (1987) reached this conclusion as a result of her work with both Palestinian and Israeli children, though she also cites evidence from the Vietnam-War period involving children from both the US and Australia. For example, she claims that among Palestinian children, those who have had personal experience of political violence are most likely to approve of war as a means of solving problems. In other words, what she suggests is that the more children and young people personally experience political violence, the more positive their attitudes towards political violence per se. Further, she also seems to believe that these attitudes will generalize to other aspects of children's lives and that such young people will find it difficult to develop strategies other than violence for solving problems. This in turn is a sentiment that Liddell et al. (1993, p. 210) note, has been echoed by several researchers in South Africa who have begun to question the 'potential of today's children to partake in peaceful negotiations for a settlement'.

And this is not a new idea. Shortly after the end of World War II (in 1950) Gillespie and Allport (1955) carried out a study involving college students from 10 different countries who were asked to write their autobiography 'from now to 2000 AD'. Some 60 per cent of these young people who had lived through World War II expected a Third World War within the next 15 years. This was despite the fact that they also saw war as 'needless and preventable'.

In contrast to this pessimism Bender and Frosch (1942) claimed that the children they studied (who were in-patients on the children's ward at Bellevue Hospital) saw peace as something to be sought after. Similarly, researchers in Northern Ireland have claimed that there is abundant evidence that whether one asks children to write essays (McWhirter, 1982), or asks them to complete the Rokeach values survey (McKernan, 1980), the overwhelming picture is one of individuals who condemn violence and see as an ideal 'a world at peace'. Similar results have been obtained in Israel (Ziv et al., 1974), in South Africa (Liddell, 1993) and in Uganda and Sudan (Dodge, 1990). What we learn from this body of research, for example, is that the single most common theme in the dreams of Israeli children was peace, that in South Africa children are more negative about violence following direct exposure, and that in Uganda and Sudan the overwhelming majority of teenagers consistently expressed the view that they were tired of war and that their main plans for the future were personal with a desire for revenge playing no part. Overall, therefore, this research evidence 'gives some cause for optimism' suggesting that if young people are 'given a meaningful alternative' to the current political violence in which they find themselves enmeshed, 'the great majority of the new generation will grasp it' (Raundalen and Dodge, 1991, p. 117).

This is a complicated issue however. One of the complications is that while children growing up in the midst of political violence may indeed grow to fear and hate war, at the same time these children may also tend to develop favourable attitudes towards fighters in their community and express a willingness to fight if necessary (Chieminti and Nasr, 1993). Part of the problem according to Punamaki is that children in countries such as Israel and Palestine, who have grown up with constant fighting and tension, find it difficult to imagine exactly what peace is. In other words, the suggestion is that such children have no representation or schema for peace. As a result these children find it difficult 'to imagine the opposite of national struggle or war/peace' (p. 69). Further, she suggests that even when they do try to imagine what peace might be, they tend to view it as something 'illusory' and 'beautiful' that has no connection to their daily life. One interesting insight into what may possibly be going on here has been offered by Rosenblatt (1983, p. 120) in his book *Children of War*. What he reports, based on his interviews with children in various societies, is that

> most of the children in the war zones patronized their parents . . . I believed that they tolerated things in their parents, like the idea of revenge, which they did not accept in the abstract or for themselves, and that they did so because they loved their parents, which they truly did, and this acceptance was a way of showing it, or because they had a small choice in the matter.

This presents a picture in which children are placed in a very difficult moral dilemma, where the adults around them, adults whom they love and cherish, favour violent solutions to political conflicts while the children themselves have come to hate and detest such violence.

Concepts of Peace and War

A useful avenue to explore, therefore, is how exactly children envisage peace and what ideas they have as to what constitutes peace. Some research has already been carried out in this area in particular in relation to the Cold War (Cooper, 1965; Tolley, 1973). What this demonstrates it that by about age 7–8 years children have developed reasonably well-defined ideas about peace and war. Ideas about peace, however, tend to involve 'negative peace' – that is a state defined simply by the absence of violence. Much less is known about childrens' ideas about 'positive peace' defined by knowledge of such concepts as 'co-operation' or harmony'.

One pioneering study which throws some light on these topics is that by Hakvoort and Oppenheimer (1993). This involved interviewing 101 middle-class Dutch children between the ages of 8 and 16 years. The interview focused on children's definition of peace and their ideas about how to make peace. All the children appeared to have acquired a comprehensive knowledge about war by 8 years. Only at age 10, however, had the same level of knowledge been acquired regarding peace. Of interest is the fact that more girls (74 per cent) than boys (43 per cent) at age 8 years had grasped the concept of peace. Girls, also, were more likely to use inter-individual ideas when trying to define peace while boys relied more on war-like terms. As predicted by earlier research all the children tended to think of peace in terms of 'negative peace'. That is they tended to conceive of peace as the absence of war or 'with a state of stillness'. Only from age 10 years on did children begin to use concepts such as human rights.

When asked to give their suggestions as to how to make peace, the vast majority of younger children made suggestions which involved solving or preventing quarrels at an individual level. Among the older children this was gradually replaced with strategies involving more global events such as preventing war between nations. However, only the girls who were interviewed, in particular the oldest (16 year-old) girls 'thought tolerance and respect between people to be an important component in any strategy to attain peace (Hakvoort and Oppenheimer, 1993, p. 71).

Unfortunately, it would appear that no study, along the lines of that just described, has been carried out involving children who have in the past been or are currently being exposed to political violence. A detailed study of the way in which children who have personally experienced political violence and the way they think about peace would be of particular interest.

Peace Education

It could also be argued, that as well as concentrating on the immediate needs of children who have been the victims of political violence psychologists ought to give more thought to preventing future political violence. One way to achieve this goal is by exposing children to what is known as 'peace education'. This is something which is already under way, at an unofficial level in some countries and in others with government backing.

The peace education movement raises several problems however. What passes as peace education can vary tremendously not only from society to society but even within societies. The most obvious problem is: what should be in the curriculum? Currently one gets the impression that many European peace education programmes (Walker, 1992) focus largely on such things as:

- the ability to resolve conflicts without resorting to violence;
- the ability to communicate including being able to express one's own views and the ability to listen to others;
- open-mindedness when dealing with those who do not hold the same views and the willingness to alter one's stance;
- the ability to try to empathize with others;
- the ability to co-operate with others and to work on tasks which require a common goal; and
- respect for others and for one's self.

In some societies, teaching about basic human rights is added to this list and, less often, material relating to international conflict. What stands out, however, is the fact that at present peace education appears to be firmly founded on the teaching of interpersonal skills which can be used to deal with interpersonal conflict. While this is no doubt a very worthy aim, it does raise a question mark over the ability of curricula such as these, to influence intergroup or political conflict – the type of conflict which most often leads to violence on a large scale. This is a problem which will be dealt with in more detail later in the chapter.

Instituting peace education in societies where conflict and perhaps also political violence are already established can be more problematic. Despite this there have been calls for peace education in countries such as South Africa where political violence has been on-going (McKendrick and Hoffman, 1990). Indeed, it has been suggested that, in societies where political violence is rife, teachers have a special responsibility to teach children the important role that they can play in rebuilding their nation within a 'political-cognitive' frame of reference. The aims of such a policy should be first to allow children to experience their world as rational and predictable (Macksoud et al., 1993). Secondly, such teaching should give children the opportunity to involve themselves intellectually and practically in putting an end to war. Finally, it should prepare young people for the future, by helping them build realistic hopes and expectations. A much less ambitious programme is at present in place in Northern Ireland where a government-sponsored programme known as Education for Mutual Understanding (EMU) and Cultural Heritage has been built into the official curriculum. The main aim of EMU is to develop links between children in their separate Catholic and Protestant schools and to emphasize 'plurality, mutual respect and tolerance of differences as well as cultural matters' (Dunn, 1993).

Sadly, peace education is often regarded as 'politically sensitive', perhaps something with a 'leftist' tinge (Walker, 1992). In certain societies it is seen as unpatriotic. Therefore, educationists planning such curricula in the future might wish to take into account an idea emanating from the work of Feshbach (1990). Feshbach claims his research indicates that there is a distinct difference between patriotism and nationalism, with the latter more strongly related to hawkish political attitudes. His suggestion is, therefore, that schools should institute programmes which teach patriotic but not nationalistic feeling. The difference, he suggests, is that:

> Patriotism entails a positive emotional relationship towards one's nation whereas nationalism reflects attitudes of or needs for superiority and power over national groups. (Feshbach, 1990, p. 191)

While this sounds like an excellent idea, a word of caution is in order. Schatz (1993) has questioned Feshbach's basic premise. He claims that, because patriotism involves distinguishing one's country from other countries, and identifying with one's country, it therefore follows in terms of Social Identity theory that patriotism will lead to nationalism, that is to positive evaluation of the in-group and negative evaluation of the out-group. Instead, he has claimed that there is a difference between what he refers to as 'blind patriotism' and 'constructive criticism'. The latter he describes as a more tolerant, flexible and questioning patriotic orientation involving a sense of responsibility for other human beings (Schatz, 1993). Obviously, therefore, while this is the germ of a good idea more empirical work is needed before deciding exactly which form of patriotism a curriculum for peace should contain.

Another, related, suggestion which merits consideration for inclusion in the peace curriculum is education focusing on analytical skills plus information access and literacy. These, according to Tiano (1986, p. 90), are 'important preconditions for the open-mindedness that counteracts authoritarianism'. Lickona (1976) goes further and suggests that, in order to develop open-mindedness, education ought to deal directly with conflicting viewpoints on social issues instead of systematically avoiding them. Garbarino et al. (1991b) suggests that children brought up in authoritarian families need to be exposed to higher-order moral reasoning in school. These issues in turn are related to the claim (discussed in chapter 3) by Garbarino and Bronfenbrenner (1976, p. 78) that 'environmental pluralism – which implies involvement in varied and increasingly complex social interactions and settings is critically important for social-moral development'.

In other words, they argue that social-moral development, which includes the ability to think in an open-minded and analytic way, is not the product of some universal motivational force but instead is the result of the interaction between the child's motivations and the particular socio-cultural milieu in which he/she is growing up. For example, they hypothesize that in societies that are dominated by a collective orientation, moral development will be arrested. At the other end of the scale, in societies in which the social order has broken down, there is likely to be an overwhelming concern for oneself. Children are then likely to grow up to become 'functionally autonomous'. Only in societies in which there are opportunities for the 'development of abstract thinking and speculation as a consequence of partially competing and overlapping allegiances' (Garbarino and Bronfenbrenner, 1976, p. 73) is a child likely to develop a principled conscience. It could, therefore, also be argued that only in such a society is a child likely to grow up able to think about issues such as war and peace in a rational way.

Is Peace Caught or Taught

Another issue that the peace movement must face therefore, is whether school is the best place for peace education to take place. Danziger (1963) noted in his study of children's future orientations that the social orientation a child is likely to adopt may depend on learning that has taken place in the family. Tolley (1973) in his study of children and the Vietnam War reported that television and newspapers were cited by children as the most important sources of knowledge. Parents, while less important where information was concerned, were an important influence on children's attitudes, feelings and opinions about the war. Research on parental responses to nuclear war may help to explain this. Work in this area has suggested that the main way that parents deal with the threat of nuclear war in relation to their children has been denial (Jacobs, 1988). Jacobs has described this as 'the ostrich effect'. What he claims is that parents do not talk to their children about the possibility of nuclear war; they therefore assume that their children know nothing about it and in this way are protected from fear. What actually happens, he believes, is that children know something about the threat of nuclear war but interpret parental silence to mean that the subject is taboo. The net effect is anything but a reduction of children's fears. Incidentally, Thompson (1986) argues that in a somewhat similar way denial may play an important role in plural societies. In such societies, he suggests, denial of the very existence of polarization is of great significance among adults and serves as a coping mechanism. While no research has apparently investigated what parents in such societies tell their children about locally-based conflict it would seem safe to assume that if they themselves deny the existence of the conflict, it is unlikely that they will discuss it with their children!

If parents have these problems discussing war and conflict with their children it is of interest to know what they tell their children about peace. This is a problem that Myers-Walls, Myers-Bowman and Pelo (1993) set out to investigate. In a small-scale study of 71 parents in the US, the parents were asked how they would respond if their child came to them and asked them what is war, what is peace and what methods they would use to teach their child about war and peace. The first two questions were open-ended, the latter was responded to using a list of eight predetermined strategies. Parent's responses to the question dealing with war were active and concrete and they often identified aspects of how war actually begins. In contrast, their responses describing peace were typically less consistent, the most common characteristic being the identification of what peace is not. What is more, the war answers were more likely than the peace answers to outline what people do. The peace answers were more likely to describe what people feel.

Myers-Walls et al. (1993) concluded that many of the parents in their study did not use developmentally appropriate techniques when talking to their children about war and peace. The problem was, they suggested, that parents tended to talk more about the abstract than the specific. If children are to be empowered to shape a future with a world at peace what is needed, in their opinion, is the possibility of children developing a representation of peace more as an activity rather than as a passive concept? This idea fits in well with Staub's (1989, p. 261) plea that parents use what he calls 'natural socialization' in order to help children to develop 'social arrangements and relations among nations' which entail 'caring, connectedness, and non-aggression'. Natural socialization, he points out involves bringing about change as a result of participation; not as a result of direct tuition. Of course, in order for parents to provide this kind of socialization the parents themselves may need appropriate education not just in terms of teaching their children about peace but in the more general techniques of child-rearing (Myers-Walls et al., 1993; Staub, 1989).

In today's western society, an important source of socialization is television. It has been suggested that television may play an important role in working against peace by helping to promote war play through advertising war-related toys. Certainly this is what one study (Costabile et al., 1992) has suggested. In a survey of parents of pre-school children carried out in England and Italy it was reported that some 40 per cent of parents indicated that their children engaged in war play and that television, along with parental attitudes and peers, were the most common sources of influence. Given the powerful influence that some believe television may have over children it is a cause for concern that for many of the world's children 'war education' may be underway well before formal peace education can even begin.

Peace educators therefore appear to overlook the fact, pointed out by Horowitz (1940) half a century ago, that for children the process of learning about other groups involves 'the development of a prejudice first and the perfection of the techniques of differentiation later'. For example, children come to value their own country above all others before they are even able to understand exactly what a country or a nation actually is (Jahoda, 1963; Piaget and Weil, 1951). Similarly, as Tajfel and his colleagues demonstrated (Tajfel, 1981) children learn first which foreign countries are 'good' or 'bad' before they learn practically anything else about them. This research calls into question the basic idea that, for example, presenting children with more facts about particular countries will alter the way they feel about these countries. This is something that appears to have been forgotten, partly because research on social cognition now dominates the field of social psychology to the extent that 'affective considerations are virtually ignored' (Pettigrew, 1986, p. 181). If the peace movement is to succeed more attention will have to be devoted to the fact that where children are concerned, emotions may play a more important role than facts.

A related question is, should children (rather than adults) be the sole focus of peace education? The obvious reason for the emphasis on children is the commonly held view that 'tomorrow's policy makers in many political, social, and economic spheres are likely to be drawn from today's students' (Burman, 1986, p. 14). However, not everyone is happy with the 'peace through children' policy. For example, it has been pointed out that, in Northern Ireland, not only are children pawns in the hands of those who wish to make war but they are also caught up in the struggles of those who wish to make peace (Cairns, 1992, p. 125). In particular, Cairns has drawn attention to the fact that in Northern Ireland there exists a substantial number of adults who feel that the way to reconcile the two communities in Northern Ireland is by first beginning with the children. Ironically what this means in reality is that there are adults who want the children of Northern Ireland to do what the adults appear unwilling to do themselves.

In a similar vein Swartz and Levett (1989, p. 747) have attacked the commonly-stated view that 'children are our future', which they claim is 'in a certain sense seriously false'. Swartz and Levett point out that the decision to focus on children is a fundamentally value-laden choice which ignores the fact that children live in a society where power is in the hands of adults and it is how this power is used that will determine the way in which children will be allowed to develop. Unfortunately too many adults appear to fool themselves into thinking that peace will be achieved only by targeting children in an attempt to nurture 'the flowering of a desocialized and reified innocent essence' (Swartz and Levett, 1989, p. 747).

What a minority of commentators have therefore argued is that peace education should be aimed at adults and in particular at sub-groups in society who have a critical role in the reduction of violence – for example the police, child-care workers and politicians. Also, it has been noted that political leaders could play an important part in the process of building for a peaceful future because, if they can model constructive conflict resolution, then violent solutions to conflict are more likely to fall into disfavour (McKendrick and Hoffmann, 1990, p. 31).

Contact

The second major strategy most commonly used to foster peace, especially with children, is based on what has come to be known as 'the contact hypothesis' (Amir, 1969). The contact hypothesis basically states that contact between people will allow them to communicate with each other and thus to discover that they share the same basic attitudes and values, and to appreciate each others' way of life. The end product of this will be positive attitudes towards each other, greater understanding and a reduction in conflict. The contact hypothesis has been around for some time and has been tested in both laboratory and field settings mainly, though not exclusively, with children. Unfortunately, despite its obvious intuitive appeal, the contact hypothesis has not received great empirical support. Moreover, even when intergroup contact takes place under what are thought to be ideal conditions, the current literature provides little evidence that intergroup contact will normally elicit more positive attitudes towards the other group as a whole.

In the 1950s the contact hypothesis contributed to social scientists' support for the desegregation of schools in the US. It is in this setting, in desegregated schools in the US, that most of the work on the contact hypothesis has been carried out. Unfortunately the results tend to have been somewhat inconsistent. Part of the problem is that the contact hypothesis can indicate how to achieve positive results when proper conditions are provided, but very rarely do schools meet the requisite conditions. Despite the fact that research in this area has been under way for nearly 50 years, specifying exactly what these requisite conditions are has become more and more difficult. As the corpus of research has grown so has the 'laundry list' of conditions needed to achieve ideal contact (Pettigrew, 1986). Today even a cursory glance at the literature will find a mention of the following factors, which are thought to be necessary for ideal contact to occur:

- authority in favour of contact;
- contact sustained not episodic;
- equal status between groups;
- initial intergroup attitudes not extremely negative;
- negative stereotypes should not be confirmed by out-group members;
- opportunity for friendship;
- personal contact on a one-to-one basis;
- pleasant social conditions;
- proportion of out-group members 50 per cent or less;
- goals should be shared;
- tolerance norms should apply; and
- voluntary basis for contact.

There has been a somewhat naïve belief in certain societies other than the US, such as Northern Ireland (Cairns, 1987) and to a lesser extent Israel and South Africa, that contact per se can alleviate conflict and indeed that the earlier that this contact takes place in an individual's life the greater the likelihood of a successful outcome. In Northern Ireland, for example, this has led to changes in the educational system including curricular initiatives, encouraging inter-school contacts and the development of new 'planned integrated schools' (Gallagher, 1992). The latter, in particular, includes as a rationale the belief that relations between members of conflicting groups can be improved by equal status contact. This is seen to be important in Northern Ireland because at present the educational system is largely segregated along religious lines.

Evidence concerning the impact of contact on attitudes in Northern Ireland is relatively limited. Some has come from short-term projects designed to bring together Catholic and Protestant children from Northern Ireland for short periods, usually in the summer. However, this evidence is beginning to indicate that short-term contact schemes may be of limited value if the sole objective is the improvement of cross-community relations; however such programs may help to improve children's individual self-esteem. More long-term contact in integrated school settings is at least likely to promote cross-community friendships. On the other hand, it appears that such contact may not radically alter children's socio-political identity (Cairns and Cairns, 1995).

Surprisingly, what the proponents of the contact hypothesis often appear to overlook is that in many of these societies there already is a degree of naturally-occurring contact. For example, Trew (1986, p. 97) has noted that although there are Catholics and Protestants in Northern Ireland who mix only with their co-religionists there is a 'sizeable minority of the population who live and work in close contact with . . . the other group'. Similarly, in South Africa white children in their pre-school years (or for longer if they live in small isolated farming communities) have traditionally mixed with black children (Foster, 1986; Nasson, 1986). Also, many white South African children have had contact with black nannies. Despite these forms of early contact most white children's attitudes towards black people are not altered to any great extent (Straker, 1990).

Contact such as this has not led to widespread change in these societies and may be linked to the other problem which has dogged research in this area – that of generalization (Hewstone and Brown, 1986). It is unusual for positive results to generalize beyond the setting in which the original contact took place, even when apparently ideal conditions can be established, and positive-attitude change is achieved. In addition, there is also a problem of generalization to other members of the out-group who were not present at the original encounter. Straker (1990, p. 180) has argued, for example, that white children's attitudes remain unchanged after contact with a black nanny because, in the white household, children are exposed to contact with black people 'in a situation which encompasses a strict hierarchy and a stratification of authority'.

This illustrates an important fact, which is that a racist society like South Africa can negate any positive effects contact might have even when that contact occurs under optimum conditions (Foster and Finchilescu, 1986). Broadly speaking, the same conclusion has been reached in Israel, where recent evidence has led some commentators to conclude that the contact hypothesis may not enhance interethnic relations in situations of political conflict (Mi'ari, 1989; Yogev, Ben-Yehoshua and Alper, 1991).

A picture is emerging, then, which suggests that the use of intergroup contact to deal with conflict is 'largely dependent on the societal structure that patterns relations between groups' (Pettigrew, 1986, p. 191). Indeed, Pettigrew has gone as far as to suggest that if it is possible to bring about the optimum conditions for contact, that is if all or most of the conditions on the 'laundry list' can be met, it usually means that the important structural issues have already worked out. In other words, what Pettigrew is saying is that the contact hypothesis may not have causal primacy.

Does this mean, therefore, that the contact hypothesis should be abandoned? In general most experts would agree that this is too extreme a position to adopt. At least it provides psychologists with the opportunity to do something. As Ben-Ari and Amir (1986) point out, in most societies, action at the micro-level is feasible whereas action at the macro-level is not usually under the control of social psychologists. Therefore, they contend that at the very least, contact leading to the reduction of conflict at the micro-level can have important effects because people have to live together even if they have not solved their political conflict. Further, improving conditions at the micro-level may, in the long-term lead to the facilitation of political or macro-level change. Also it is important to remember that the contact theory is a 'living idea' that continues to inspire research, and for this reason alone it is valuable (Stephan and Brigham, 1985).

Intergroup Contact

If one believes that contact still has a part to play in the peace process then an important issue for researchers is how the problems noted above can be overcome. Part of the problem may be that for too long we have assumed that Piaget (1934; 1987, p. 7) was correct when he suggested that 'to educate children for peace we need to . . . free . . . [them] . . . from initial egocentrism'. In other words we have for too long tended to see peace education as an individual process rather than as a group-based phenomenon.

A group-based approach is important, according to Hewstone and Brown (1986), because the lack of generalization following contact is due to contact with an out-group member taking the form of an interpersonal rather than an intergroup encounter. Hewstone and Brown (1986, p. 15) see this distinction between interpersonal and intergroup behaviour as important not just for a proper understanding of how the contact hypothesis should work, but also as 'fundamental to intergroup relations in general'.

Following Social Identity Theory (see chapter 1), Hewstone and Brown (1986) insists that there is a fundamental difference between interpersonal and intergroup processes. It follows, therefore, that intergroup processes cannot be explained, let alone altered, by focusing on interpersonal processes.

The problem is that in many contact situations, individuals while interacting as individuals do not see out-group members as exemplars of the out-group. The outcome of this is the state of affairs encapsulated in the remark 'some of my best friends are blacks/Catholics/Jews' etc. In other words, positive contact with an individual does not alter how the out-group is represented, but rather means that individuals are seen as exceptions.

In order to avoid this, Hewstone and Brown (1986) argue that for contact to be totally effective it must take place at an intergroup level. This means that out-group members taking part must be seen as group representatives rather than individuals. If this is not accomplished, they warn, any positive outcomes will be 'primarily cosmetic'.

Paradoxically, therefore, part of the solution may be to make people's group affiliations more salient in the contact situation and not less salient (Brown, 1988), thereby ensuring that the participants see each other as representative of their groups and not merely as exceptions to the rule. In this way, contact-based schemes should ideally aim to change people's minds about what constitutes a typical group member (Werth and Lord, 1992).

Of course such views are easy to express and relatively easy to bring about in the controlled conditions of a social psychology experiment. However, insuring that such changes can take place in more naturally occurring situations is more difficult. Part of the difficulty is that the impressions that we form of a group will depend on the situations under which we sample that group's behaviour. The problem here is that while some contact settings will permit the expression of the particular behaviour that we want to disconfirm we cannot be sure that this will always happen. For example, if the particular stereotype is that the out-group is lazy, then finding situations in which members of the out-group are working hard will not be difficult. But what if the stereotype is untrustworthy/devious/sly/treacherous? These are just the sort of traits that real-life groups in conflict often ascribe to each other. It is much more difficult to find contact settings which permit the expression of behaviours which will disconfirm beliefs such as these.

Another issue is, on how many occasions do we have to see the out-group as not being lazy, for example, for our stereotype 'the out-group is lazy' to be disconfirmed?

Finally a major problem, is how to ensure that contact with typical out-group members is not destructive rather than constructive. Obviously those who organize such activities are only too aware that if stereotypical out-group members are involved there is the distinct danger that stereotypes will simply be confirmed rather that altered.

For reasons such as this, the most recent thinking is that for contact to disconfirm key stereotypic beliefs it must not only involve intergroup contact but also involve contact with a member or members of the out-group. This member should be prototypical in all respects with the exception of the one key factor to be disconfirmed. Further, the contact should take place over a long period of time and in order for the specific disconfirming stereotyped behaviour or belief to be expressed the contact should actually take place under highly structured conditions in which, perhaps, the interactions should actually be scripted (Desforges et al., 1991).

Changing Intergroup Boundaries

It is important, not to give the impression that contact is the only way psychological research suggests intergroup conflict can be overcome. There is research which suggests that contact is not actually necessary in order to alter stereotypes (Gaertner et al., 1990). Changes in stereotypic beliefs can come about by indirect means, such as changes in social norms, changes in the law, as well as changes in images promulgated by gatekeepers such as the media. In 1936 Horowitz pointed out that among the white children he was studying 'attitudes towards Negroes are chiefly determined not by contact with Negroes, but by contact with the prevalent attitudes toward Negroes' (p. 34).

Social identity theorists therefore, tend not to advocate contact as the primary way of attacking intergroup conflict. The approach that they most strongly advocate involves efforts to manipulate the intergroup context either in an attempt to eliminate intergroup boundaries or to make them less salient. Wilder (1986) has been among the leading proponents of this approach and has suggested several ways in which the impact of social categorization can be weakened or diverted. In general three types of strategies have been advanced. First of all there are attempts to lessen the psychological distance between groups, secondly there are attempts to remove intergroup boundaries entirely, and thirdly there are attempts to remove conflict by encouraging the creation of a superordinate category.

None of these ideas is of itself especially original. What interests psychologists is to test the effectiveness of each and to try to find out why. For example, research which has tried to diminish the psychological distance between groups has focused on the role of contextual factors – specifically the presence of another out-group which serves as a comparison or reference point (Wilder and Thompson, 1980). This suggests that the existence of a more extreme out-group can serve as an anchor point which causes the first out-group to be judged as less different from the in-group.

The second approach is that of removing intergroup boundaries entirely. Here research has tended to centre on the role of intergroup co-operation. Co-operation, it is suggested, may reduce the salience of intergroup boundaries and in certain circumstances may remove that boundary entirely by inducing group members to conceive of themselves as one group rather than as two separate groups (Gaertner et al., 1990). In this area attempts are currently under way to discover which elements of co-operation are necessary for this to happen. Is, for example, interaction important; or is it the focus on common problems/goals; or is common fate between group members crucial; or is cross-cutting necessary? That is, do members have to work in mixed teams on a co-operative task or is it better for role assignments to subtasks to converge with existing social categories? Early indications are that research is favouring the latter approach in which cross-cutting is not employed (Marcus-Newhall et al., 1993).

Finally, there is the possibility of inducing a superordinate category. This would mean that the existing group boundaries are left intact but that members of both groups recognize at the same time that they are members of a higher order category.

The ultimate solution is trying to alter, perhaps even eliminate, the categorization process itself. This is a radical and long-term alternative which suggests that something should be done to reduce the amount of social categorization to which people resort. One might hypothesize that this could be achieved. It would need to involve young children, teaching them to think of people as individuals and not as members of social categories and indeed some of the peace education programs noted earlier incorporate this idea.

However, almost certainly this is a pious hope which is bound to fail. All the research indicates that categorization is an important and normal process. Rather than waste time trying to alter this essential psychological process, therefore, it would be much better to learn how to alter the content of stereotypes instead of trying to eliminate stereotyping entirely.

Summary

One of the problems, it has been suggested, in bringing peace to societies that have experienced political violence, is that the the next generation will have either begun to believe that there is no future, or that they will be able to think of the future only in negative terms. Fortunately, while this may be true in some societies it is not inevitable. Further, it is clear that this is not simply an all or none phenomenon. Much depends on what is happening in child's society at the time and perhaps more importantly what is happening to his/her group in that society. If that group's influence is on the wane the child may have a less rosy view of the future.

At present these views are based on excellent evidence with data collected over many years using exemplary methodology. What is not known is how safe it is to generalize from this research (which has virtually all been carried out in South Africa). It is therefore important that these studies should be replicated in other societies.

In the absence of such a replication one could hazard a guess that results from other countries will not be too different. This means that it is possible to explore children's views about the future in more detail. Especially it means that we should be asking 'are children directly exposed to political violence able to envisage peace in the future or have their experiences turned them into perpetual war-mongers?'

Before we reach a satisfactory answer to this question, however, we need find a systemtatic way to ask these questions. Fortunately this research has now begun. The next step will be to compare children who live in peaceful societies with children exposed directly to political violence.

Given that we know little about the way in which children develop concepts of peace and war it could be argued that it is premature to try to educate children to be peace-makers. Despite this lack of basic knowledge this process has already begun in some societies and some people apparently believe it is effective. However, there is virtually no empirical evidence to substantiate their claim. A major problem would appear to be that too much of what passes for peace education focuses on interpersonal conflict as opposed to intergroup conflict. In future curriculum designers need to produce a more effective peace education program and also to overcome the problem that peace education per se is not always politically acceptable.

It could also be argued that school-based peace education is always bound to be ineffective because it targets the wrong people in the wrong setting. For example there is speculation, if not evidence, that children's ideas about peace and war may be more influenced by what they learn from their parents than from their schools. There is definitely evidence, which is now often forgotten, that learning about such things as peace and war involves emotions primarily and that providing facts may not alter these emotions. This is obviously an area in need of much more research, in order to develop what is known and make it amenable for use in applied settings.

The alternative to peace education which is most often advocated is bringing children together from opposing groups in order to foster positive intergroup attitudes – the contact hypothesis. This has been a well-researched area for many years and now boasts an extensive literature. What this literature indicates is that for contact to be even minimally effective it has to take place under highly prescribed conditions. However what advocates of the contact hypothesis appear reluctant to accept is that while there is evidence that bringing groups together promotes interpersonal contact satisfactorily it does not necessarily promote intergroup contact.

There is also good evidence that intergroup conflict can reduced by manipulating the process of social categorization in order to alter group boundaries. This is a strategy that both social scientists and policy makers should consider more often. The evidence also suggests it is not possible to bring social categorization to an end entirely. Rather it is better to better to concentrate on altering the content of stereotypes or manipulating who gets put in which social category by altering intergroup boundaries.

6 Overview

The aim of this book has been to make research on children and political violence available to a wider audience in the hope that this in turn will lead to further research. The aim, however, has not simply been to provide an uncritical review of the literature. Instead I have tried to emphasize strengths and weaknesses in existing knowledge, and beginning in chapter 1 have tried to make the reader aware of the methodological problems faced by researchers in this area. In this closing chapter I will again concentrate on methodological issues first, while attempting to summarize what has been learned from the preceding pages. Before doing this it is necessary to repeat that relatively little research has been carried out in this area despite the fact that research has been going on for at least half a century. Today, however, a slow and uneven growth is underway.

A major problem is that the two key concepts, children and political violence, are both in effect social constructions and therefore both are difficult to define. To accommodate this a broad definition of childhood as lasting from birth to late teens was adopted, while political violence was defined simply as 'acts of an intergroup nature seen by both sides or one to constitute violent behaviour'.

While the breadth of these definitions is necessary because of the underdeveloped state of the field they do not make it any easier to bring together what is a very disparate literature.

Universal Model of Childhood

To begin with what this literature reveals is that instead of facing up to this problem researchers tend to assume a 'universal decontextualized model of child development' (Dawes and Donald, 1994).

That is, researchers tend to forget that 'childhood, adolescence and adulthood are . . . socially defined statuses which include social expectations that differ across cultures' (Roe, 1994). All of this becomes important when we consider a whole range of issues from the symptoms that children may experience to their active participation in political movements.

For example, we in the West react with horror at the sight on our television screens of boy-soldiers. What we have to remember, is that while we see these boys as children and so deserving of special treatment, this perception may well say more about us that it does about the plight of the children we are watching.

Universal Contexts

Similarly most researchers duck the issue of comparability of contexts. Instead there is an assumption that because two or more particular locations have been labelled on the television news as 'war-torn' Belfast and, for example, 'war-torn' Beirut, that conditions for children growing up there are identical. Political violence can mean different things. For example, it may mean all-out civil war or civil disturbances. Should it be assumed that each of these has the same impact on children?

In much of this book I have used the phrase 'children exposed to political violence'. What is not clear, however, is: were the children equally exposed and what is the metric that should be employed? This is because even when it can be established that researchers are talking about exactly the same form of political violence, can it be assumed that all children were equally exposed? For example, not all children who live in either Belfast or Beirut will have been equally exposed to the violence. Some may be exposed to many minor incidents and rather fewer perhaps to just one major incident. How are these differences to be accounted for?

A good example of the importance of the wider socio-political context has been provided by Straker et al. (1996). She compared the results of three studies in South Africa all carried out in the same township with children of the same age. The first study was undertaken during 1986 when young people were in open conflict with the state, the second in 1989 when state repression was at its height, and the third during 1992 when state repression had been abandoned and intra-community feeling was rampant.

One question that was common to all three of these studies was 'what makes living in a township hard?'. When the proportion of respondents answering 'violence' was calculated the results were 9 per cent (1986), 2 per cent (1989) and 76 per cent (1992). In other words, many more young people reported that violence was a hardship in 1992 than in either of the other two years. This Straker et al. (1996) suggests is because the violence in the early years was 'clearly linked to a struggle for liberation'. Because of this, they suggest that it was construed differently and experienced less negatively in earlier years.

Put simply then, the problem is, when authors from around the world state that they are investigating 'the impact of political violence on children', can we be sure they are talking about exactly the same phenomenon impacting in exactly the same way on identical subjects?

Stress and Coping

The literature on children and political violence is dominated by work on stress and coping. One might claim this is the topic where research is most advanced. However even on this topic the existing work can be difficult to interpret and is a methodological minefield.

All of this is not helped by the fact that faced with children suffering from the results of political violence, researchers have tended to adopt a somewhat short-sighted approach which focuses only on children's relatively short-term needs. Because of this, much of the research in this area could be accused of simply providing a 'scientifically respectable basis for moral outrage' (Swartz and Levett, 1989).

Is Traumatization Inevitable?

This appears to have passed unnoticed outside the specialized research community where it is apparently seen as inevitable that every child who is exposed to political violence will suffer serious psychological consequences. The one unambiguous conclusion that can be reached from the literature reviewed in chapter 2, however, is that such suffering is not inevitable. For example, if two children are exposed to exactly the same incident and one is severely traumatized, it is not certain that the other will suffer at all.

Actual Symptoms

The children who do suffer sufficiently to be considered clinically ill display a wide variety of symptoms. So wide is the range of symptoms that it probably serves no useful purpose trying to list them here. A more useful development has been the tendency in recent studies to apply the criteria for PTSD. As a result this diagnosis has become more common. Perhaps the most salient characteristic is that among those who suffer severely (compared with those who suffer 'normal' levels of anxiety) symptoms tend to become worse with time, not better.

Coping

The fact that at least some children are resilient, even when exposed to the horrors of political violence, has led to a search for those factors which may differentiate children who escape the more severe forms of stress and those who do not. At first the spotlight focused on personal factors such as age, sex and personality. However, very few studies have examined these personal factors in any systematic way and as a result it is impossible to draw any clear conclusions.

For example, despite many hypotheses as to which age group will suffer most there is no clear evidence in this area. Even the results concerning sex differences are contradictory. Also, the long-accepted dictum that anxious children are more vulnerable when exposed to political violence actually receives only minimal empirical support. In fact, one of the best studies in this area by Milgram and Milgram (1976) suggests that the opposite may be true. The difficulty here is that researchers have tended to investigate these variables in isolation. What is needed is more research which investigates the interaction of age, sex and personality in relation to resilience among children exposed to political violence.

Social support: Since the early work in Britain during World War II it has been accepted that the effects of political violence on children can be mediated by social support, with the extended family, the child's peers, and the wider community all being seen as potential sources of such support. These sources of social support have however attracted only anecdotal speculation. Most of the empirical work has operationally defined social support as the presence of one or both parents (but especially the presence of the child's mother).

While it is undoubtedly true that parents, especially the mother, can play such a role, the circumstances in which the child's family can serve to protect the child psychologically are now seen to be more limited than earlier claims would have led one to expect. This is because it is now recognized that parents may themselves find it increasingly difficult to function normally as the level of political violence increases. Also there are suggestions in the more recent literature that the relationship between the child's level of functioning and that of his/her parents is a complex one involving not simply mother and child health levels, but also, for example, the coping patterns adopted by both mother and child.

Despite the fact that the empirical evidence in this area is growing, a major weakness remains the way in which the child's psychological health tends to be assessed. At present much of the research confounds mother-and-child health levels, because the mother is the source of information for both.

Appraisal: One way forward, that was suggested in chapter 2, may be to make more use of the Lazarus and Folkman cognitive-phenomenological model. According to this model the psychological outcome of a stressful experience depends on the way the stressor is evaluated (appraisal) and the strategy used to deal with it (coping).

Surprisingly no research appears to have adopted this model with children exposed to political violence. In particular, there is little information about the way in which children appraise various forms of political violence, or what factors influence this appraisal process. There is some weak evidence that the child's religious and political beliefs may influence the appraisal process but much more work is needed. Also, virtually nothing is known about the way in which children obtain information about on-going political violence; for example, what do their parents tell them, and how do they evaluate what they are told?

Rather more has been written about the coping processes that children may be using, with denial/distancing and/or habituation receiving a good deal of attention. This evidence is hard to evaluate because, while denial/distancing and habituation are interesting ideas and worthy of further research, a major problem is that both concepts are difficult to define operationally. Indeed some investigators have argued that what has been interpreted as distancing/denial is in fact habituation. On balance what empirical evidence there is would appear to support this position.

Long-term effects: The largest single source of evidence in this area comes from Holocaust survivors. Initially, research in this area claimed that difficulties in later life were universal among this population. More recent, and better research is beginning to suggest that these claims were exaggerated. Similarly, the recent evidence which focuses on children who become refugees is mildly optimistic, at least in the medium term. In particular the child's pre-refugee family support is emerging as an important factor. These conclusions must, however, for the moment remain based on weak evidence. Studies in this area tend to lack adequate (or any) control groups, while samples are often biased because they are obtained from clinical sources.

Stress and Coping: Methodology

Despite the fact that research in this area has been underway for at least fifty years the field is still beset with methodological problems. Too many researchers give the impression that they feel that theirs is the first or one of the first studies to be carried out in this area, and for this reason methodological niceties can be ignored.

Research designs: Some of these methodological problems are of course endemic to the area, especially those which influence the actual research designs that are adopted. For example there are still very few studies in which children have been evaluated both before and after their exposure to political violence. This is understandable given the difficulty in predicting where incidents will occur and the ethical issues involved. However, there is no such excuse for the studies which either do not employ a control group or employ inadequate controls. Nor is it clear why more research does not follow-up children seen when violence is at its height, at a later time when the violence may have subsided.

Measurement: A major problem is that research is usually done by different researchers employing different measurement techniques in different parts of the world. It is therefore difficult to tell if different researchers are in fact measuring the same thing. The obvious answer to this problem, it would appear, is research carried out using exactly the same instruments in different countries with children who have been exposed to exactly the same form of political violence.

But is the solution so simple? It is highly likely that there are cultural differences in the way children react emotionally to the stress of political violence. What people experience as traumatic is not a cultural universal (Ingleby, 1988). Researchers using, therefore, an identical questionnaire in two very different societies – even if the issues of linguistic equivalence, etc., have been taken care of – cannot be sure that they are measuring the same thing. On the other hand, developing ecologically valid measures in separate societies will in turn again raise problems of cross-cultural comparability.

More complex models: At present the field tends to be dominated by extremely simplistic one-shot studies. Hopefully future studies will allow more sophisticated mutivariate models to be tested. In this respect a useful starting place for future researchers is the model outlined by Gibson (1989). This model emphasizes the fact that the effects of stress should be perceived as part of an 'on-going process of person-situation interaction over time'. If Gibson's model is adopted, researchers would need to acquire information as to the specific-immediate stressful events children have been exposed to (level 1). Also information concerning intra-personal factors including sex, age, personality, coping style, educational attainment would be needed (level 2). To this would be added data on interpersonal factors such as family and other sources of social support (level 3). Finally the wider context including social, political and economic factors would be taken into account (level 4).

While it is possible at present to find research that has examined the moderating role of each of these factors on its own, few studies have examined the interaction of all four factors.

Social identity and coping: Future research may also wish to consider the possibility that in contexts of political violence children's social identities can play a role in moderating the impact of stress. This is because it is highly likely that the groups a child identifies with may determine whether an act of political violence is regarded positively or negatively. If future research takes social identity into account it may help to reject the 'crude' idea that somehow children are always psychologically compelled to 'bring their experience of abuse and violence to bear on their future relations in a negative manner' Dawes (1994a, p. 195), while illustrating the close links between social identity, coping politics and indeed morality (see below).

In addition there is the possibility that social identity can be harnessed to help with long-term coping. For example, in post-war Japan becoming an 'economic soldier' was the way that young men who had felt the war's devastation most acutely claimed a future when faced with national defeat (Elder and Meguro, 1987).

Stress, coping and medical discourse: Before leaving the topic of stress and coping it is necessary to record that there are those writers who object to the use of the terms 'stress and coping' in relation to children and political violence. These terms they claim indicate a primarily medical discourse in which children are seen as 'ill' and professionals as people who will provide treatment. This leads to two problems. At one level there is the simple issue of whether to intervene or not in order to help those children exposed to political violence. Schwarzwald (1993, p. 408) has for example claimed that as time usually leads to an 'evaporation' of stress reactions there is the distinct possibility that 'professional intervention may make an issue of a problem that would dissipate by itself'. (Incidentally, the same perhaps could be said for research and may account for the reluctance of parents and teachers to allow children to become involved in research projects in this area as noted in chapter 2.)

A second objection is that use of these terms forces children into the role of passive 'victims' which in turn leads to 'secondary dependency upon helpers' (Foster, 1989). This approach, according to its critics, makes the mistake of assuming that psychological trauma is analogous to physical trauma. This mechanistic analogy, they claim, will not hold because in the case of children, the 'object' which has been subjected to trauma is able to 'engage with it intelligently and socially' (Dawes, 1994a).

Everyday Life, Aggression and Morality

The biggest impact political violence may have on children may not necessarily be a psychological one. Political violence can damage the general infrastructure of society and thus disrupt everything from the necessities of life – by interrupting food supplies – to medical services. Also political violence can bring with it an increased risk of accidental injury or death.

Family Life, School and Play

The impact of political violence on family life has seldom come under scrutiny despite the obvious fact that as a result of political violence the whole family structure may come under pressure, even where the family remains intact. One suggestion is that this may lead to changes in such basic things as parental child-rearing tactics. In addition it has been speculated that these changes may in turn influence the way in which the next generation bring up their children. However, despite the importance of this area, the amount of hard evidence concerning the family and its role in mediating the impact of political violence is almost negligible.

Likewise the role of schools and schooling as a mediator of political violence has received only a minimum of attention. There is anecdotal evidence indicating that if schools can be kept open they may act to protect children, but this has not been confirmed empirically. What is clear is that, at least in developed countries, political violence can disrupt children's education.

Play is considered an essential activity if children are to develop normally and indeed some observers see play as a therapeutic activity. One concern, therefore, has been that in societies where political violence exists children will be unable or unwilling to play. What evidence there is, suggests that on the contrary political violence can be stimulating for children even though it is true that such play may well involve significant physical danger.

A common assertion from societies where political violence prevails is that children are not only stimulated to play, but actually incorporate features of the outside world, particularly its aggressiveness into their play. This idea has been tested empirically but no clear results have emerged. Therefore, while it is clear that play exposes children to physical dangers, it is not clear whether the actual content of that play is greatly influenced by on-going political violence.

Socio-economic status

While we know virtually nothing about the impact of political violence on children's family life, on their school performance, or on the way they play, we do know with some certainty that the everyday problems of childhood do not vanish with the onset of political violence. All the disadvantages normally associated with lower socio-economic status remain.

Indeed, the research, while limited, does suggest that there may be a cumulative effect with the direct negative consequences of political violence added to or interacting with the effects of economic and social disadvantage. For example, faced with political violence it is likely to be the poorer families who are less likely to flee or are less likely to be able to afford food at black-market prices.

It could be argued, therefore, that among western researchers in particular, what has not been understood is that the impact of political violence on children is not primarily a psychological phenomenon. Instead, as a UNICEF document of 1984 pointed out, issues such as the 'long war on poverty and underdevelopment', and the struggle for such things as women's rights, land reform, disarmament, and a more equitable international order 'remain fundamental determinants of children's survival, health and well-being' (p. 16).

Because this has not been understood there has been a tendency to 'psychologize' the problem. Not surprisingly it is from psychologists outside North America, psychologists actually living as well as working in societies where political violence exists, that the call for the need to avoid 'psychologizing' the issue of children and political conflict has come first. For example, Dawes (1990) in South Africa has noted that even such apparently obvious issues as the degree of violent behaviour among young people in a society caught up in political violence 'is not likely to be a simple function' of the young people's involvement in the political struggle. Instead, he suggests that a more fundamental cause may be exposure to a culture of survival in a setting of economic deprivation and political repression.

Depsychologizing the problem: Western psychology is at present not in a good position to meet this challenge for several reasons. One of these is the trend towards increasing specialization in the discipline. This presents a major problem when attempting to tackle social issues such as poverty, racism or political conflict, because these are problems whose 'roots are multifaceted', and which require 'analysis through broad perspectives' (Moghaddam, 1990, p. 36). So one challenge for the future is that psychologists should co-operate with scholars from other disciplines such as economics and politics. Nor is co-operating with other disciplines the only challenge facing psychologists who care for the future of the world's children threatened by political violence. As the discipline of psychology grows ever more fragmented there is also a need for psychologists to co-operate with other psychologists.

Such a change in emphasis is, according to Moghaddam, already under way in some Third World societies and will, he believes, lead to the development of a more indigenous psychologys. These indigenous psychologys he feels will in turn almost inevitably result in a degree of 'despecialization' which in turn may have implications for mainstream psychology.

Aggression

Adult observers have tended to report that political violence increases aggression in real life as well as in play, for example in interactions with peers. This happens, it is suggested either because children are modelling themselves on the adults around them or because aggressive behaviour is a form of coping.

Three well-designed studies have looked at this question but each has reached a different conclusion. Two concluded that there is evidence that political violence increases aggressive behaviour. The first of these (Chiementi et al., 1989) claimed to have found a definite relationship, while the second (Liddell et al., 1996) found a relationship but suggested that it was much more subtle. Finally the most recent study (Farver and Frosch, 1996) found no evidence for any relationship.

Evaluating the evidence in this area is difficult because, as is often the case, no two studies were exactly the same. As a result, despite the unusually high quality of evidence available, no clear conclusions can be reached. If nothing else, this illustrates the urgent need for cross-national replication of research in this area, a topic that will be returned to later.

Moral Development

There is much anecdotal evidence, but only weak empirical evidence, that children's moral attitudes and values may be modified by exposure to political violence. Also it is unfortunate that most of the empirical evidence comes from one society only – Northern Ireland. There, it has been concluded, based on research using measures of moral reasoning, that children may have an underdeveloped sense of the complexity of moral problems. This needs to be confirmed in other societies.

Further, when moral attitudes have been examined (measured using paper and pencil tests) no effect of political violence has been found.

Crime

On the other hand, it is very clear that, at least in developed societies, juvenile crime increases with increasing political violence. Despite the unequivocal demonstration of this phenomenon, there is no evidence to suggest that permanent changes in moral standards are responsible. Instead, the most likely explanation is that such behaviour is related to the absence of authority figures, such as fathers and/or the police, combined with extreme economic deprivation. This conclusion is reinforced by evidence which suggests that any long-term effects in this area are probably minimal.

Crime, moral development and social identity: It appears, therefore, that both aggressiveness and juvenile crime may increase in children exposed to political violence, yet there is no evidence that political violence has any impact on moral reasoning. At first glance this appears to be contradictory. Part of the problem arises, however, because the connection between actual behaviour and moral reasoning is a complex one. The initial research in this area set a trend which continues today, which minimized the influence of the environment on the child's understanding of what is just (Bronfenbrenner, 1962), and in doing so probably missed the point that what such research was really tapping was children's knowledge of the norms that operate in his/her culture. This in turn means that because morality is shaped by culture as well as individual experiences 'different people may arrive at different moral decisions even when they rely on the same formal principles' (Nissan and Koriat, 1989, p. 214). Therefore, whether the behaviour of individual children exposed to political violence will be altered or not may depend not so much on their individual cognitive processes but rather on the norms of the groups to which they belong.

A clue to understanding which moral standards apply in which situations may lie in Social Identity Theory. This theory suggests that how we think about ourselves tends to vary along a continuum, from the perception of self as a unique person where we see ourselves as very different from other individuals, to the perception of the self as very similar or identical to in-group members and very different from out-group members.

This means that in certain situations we can come to perceive ourselves as the interchangeable exemplars of a particular social category rather than as a unique personality. This phenomenon Turner (1987) has labelled depersonalization. It is because of depersonalization that we come to act as members of groups.

What is being suggested here is that in personal situations personal moral standards will apply but in group or intergroup situations the morality of the group applies. Dawes (1994b, p. 213) has used these ideas convincingly to argue this point in the context of South Africa. In particular, he has suggested that certain group identities can help to prohibit or sanction forms of behaviour regardless of the ability of the individual members of the group to reason at a certain level of abstraction about moral problems.

This area merits further exploration along with the theoretical ideas of Garbarino and Bronfenbrenner (1976) which attempt to link culture to moral development. These ideas in turn could also be related to questions about children's active involvement in politics.

Political Activists

It is important to remember that 'a developing child is both a mechanism and a social agentic creature, and that both lenses are necessary to appreciate the whole' (Dawes, 1994a). Perhaps, as noted earlier, because of the domination of the medical model, the literature virtually always portrays children as the passive victims of political violence (Foster, 1986). The evidence however, as outlined in chapter 4, indicates instead that children can be active participants in political violence.

What, Who and Why?

So far three basic questions have dominated the literature – in what way are children involved in politics, are these children different from other children and why do they become politically active?

The most common form of political activity that children are involved in is rioting and demonstrating of various kinds. This is a relatively peripheral activity which according to media reports may involve quite young children. Exceptionally, for example in South Africa and Palestine, this form of activity may involve a majority of young people, and their role can become more central to the political struggle. Limited evidence suggests that only a minority of all children ever become involved in these activities and that those involved are probably older than the media likes to suggest.

A second way that a very small number of young people become politically active is by joining terrorist organizations and/or liberation armies where they may be involved at the margins, for example, carrying messages or more directly in killing.

A wide range of suggestions have been made to explain why

children become involved in rioting and protesting. For example, there is the possibility that they are modelling themselves on adult behaviour, or that they value the thrill of danger, or that these activities are an extension of gang-related activities common at this age. A worrying suggestion is that adult involvement may be more overt – the Godfather hypothesis – or that adults, especially parents, condone if not approve of this behaviour. At present there are no definite answers to these questions.

The children who join paramilitary groups or guerrilla armies are probably slightly older than their stone-throwing brothers and sisters. The groups they join can be categorized into one of two types – anarchic/ideologues and nationalist/separatists. More children and young people probably join the latter.

The favoured explanation for this behaviour has been that terrorist/guerrilla organizations attract a disproportionate number of psychopathic individuals. However, there is relatively good evidence that the vast majority of children and young people who join nationalist/separatist guerrilla movements are not psychopaths.

Also, it is clear that it is difficult to fit these young people into any particular socio-demographic or psychological categories. There is minimal evidence to support the common claim that there is a particular 'terrorist type'. What is more, it could be argued that 'terrorist personality types', or psychodynamic explanations for involvement in terrorism, will always be very hard to verify.

At a more basic level it has been suggested that rewards such as prestige, glamour, excitement and even material rewards may play a role in attracting young people to paramilitary groups. However, while material rewards may function to sustain membership in such organizations it is not clear if these are the reasons people join in the first place.

One suggestion is that young people choose to join paramilitary groups because of the way in which they have been socialized. This socialization, it is suggested, may take place in fairly subtle ways, particularly via the indirect impact of such institutions as the family, or in schools. In these settings the teaching of history either formally or informally may play an important role.

An interesting hypothesis, which is supported by some qualitative evidence, is that being a victim or watching another person become a victim may play a role in encouraging young people to become involved in politics in this way. While this is an interesting hypothesis it is difficult to obtain hard evidence to support it. The small amount of evidence there is has often been obtained by journalists rather than social scientists. Further, the sources that journalists have used are not obtained from random samples of terrorists. Therefore, what we know has come largely from conversations with those who have left their organization, for example, because they have renounced its aims or because they have been apprehended and detained by their opponents.

Of course, not all young people who are involved in political violence are in illegal organizations. There are still many state-run armies around the world that include children in their ranks and indeed a recent estimate suggests that about one-third of the armed forces of NATO are aged 18 years or under.

Regardless of which organization a child or young person becomes a member of, it is likely that they will be taught to kill. In many of these organizations it appears that the recruitment period may be used as an indoctrination phase in preparation for this event. To begin with the new recruit is asked to take part in relatively innocuous activities and these gradually escalate, which allows moral disengagement to take place.

A common fear in many post-conflict societies is that young people who have been trained to kill and perhaps to defy the forces of law and order will never be able to abandon this role. In many ways this is related to the debate above on morality. Anecdotal evidence suggests, however, that antisocial behaviour is not likely to generalize to everyday life. One explanation for this may be that a key element in membership of paramilitary groups is the development of a morality based on group loyalty.

Political Behaviour, Morality and Social Identity

This in turn suggests a link between politics, morality and social identity, because it appears that the 'socio-political and the moral contexts interlock as group interests become salient' (Dawes, 1994b). An outstanding, if chilling example of this is the case reported by Fanon (1967, p. 217–19) in which, during their country's struggle for liberation, two Algerian boys (aged 13 and 14 years) were accused of having killed their European school-friend.

When questioned the younger boy told Fanon that 'he was a good friend of ours [but] we decided to kill him because the Europeans wanted to kill all the Arabs. We can't kill big people. But we could kill ones like him.'

The older boy, gave a more overtly political answer. When asked 'tell me why you killed this boy who was your friend', he replied, 'I'll tell you why. You've heard of the Rivet business'. Rivet was a village where Europeans had massacred Algerians.

As Engestrom (1988), who has analyzed the conversations with Fanon in some detail, notes, the boys' behaviour appears irrational when looked at in terms of individual actions. However, seen in terms of 'collective action' the behaviour makes more sense. In particular what Social Identity Theory would suggest is that this is an example of children behaving as group members and therefore perceiving their friend not as an individual but as a representative of another group, in fact as one of 'them', the enemy.

The Fanon example illustrates not only how children may come to behave in ways that in other circumstances they would view as immoral, but also indicates how children may become involved in what to the adult world at least is political behaviour. This is another area where research is badly needed. Indeed, it has been suggested that we 'understand less about the process of political socialization today than we did (or thought we did) ten or fifteen years ago' (Cook, 1985). Again this is an area where Social Identity Theory may at least help to stimulate such research.

Promoting Peace

Some gloomy reports have suggested that children who have experienced political violence either start to believe that there is no future, or are able to think of the future only in negative terms. If this were true this might significantly influence the peace-making capabilities of future generations.

This is one area where there is excellent evidence, which includes data collected over many years. What this evidence indicates is that while children in some societies exposed to political violence may become less confident about what the future holds, this is not inevitable. Also it has become clear that the view children take of the future depends on what is happening in the child's society at the time, and perhaps more importantly what is happening to his/her group in that society. If, for example, that group's influence is on the wane, the child is more likely to hold a gloomy view of the future.

What we do not know is if it is safe to generalize from this work, which has virtually all been carried out in South Africa, to other societies. These are yet more important studies that need to be replicated cross-nationally.

Also future research should try to explore children's views about the future in more detail. In particular we should be asking: are children directly exposed to political violence able to envisage peace in the future, or have their experiences turned them into perpetual warmongers? To begin this process we need answers to even more basic questions such as: what do children understand by the terms peace and war?

Some research asking these questions has begun but so far it has been confined to children who have not been exposed to political violence. What is now needed is work which explores the possibility that experiencing political violence directly influences children's ideas about what constitutes peace and how it can be achieved.

Peace Education

When we know more about the way in which children develop concepts of peace and war, and whether these are altered by the experience of political violence, then we will be in a better position to try to educate children to be peace-makers. At present there appears to be virtually no empirical evidence to substantiate the claim that peace education is at all effective. One reason for this may be that peace education focuses too much on interpersonal conflict as opposed to intergroup conflict. Finally, for peace education to be effective it also needs to overcome the hurdle of becoming politically acceptable – which at present is not the case in many societies.

Another argument is that school is the wrong place to carry out peace education. There is speculation, if not evidence, that children's ideas about peace and war may be the product of what they learn from their parents rather than from their schools. This in turn may be related to the fact that learning about such things as peace and war primarily involves emotions, and that providing facts may not alter these emotions. For these reasons it could be argued that peace education should be aimed at adults (especially parents) rather than at children.

Intergroup Approaches

The alternative to formal peace education which is most often advocated is bringing children together from opposing groups in order to foster positive intergroup attitudes. This is known as the contact hypothesis and has been a well-researched area for many years. Research on this topic indicates that even if contact is only to be minimally effective it has to take place under highly prescribed conditions. Further, while there is evidence that bringing groups together promotes interpersonal contact satisfactorily the same evidence also suggests that it does not necessarily promote intergroup contact.

There is also good evidence that intergroup conflict can be reduced by manipulating group boundaries and both social scientists and policy makers should consider this strategy more often. Another strategy sometimes advocated is to attempt to bring social categorization to an end entirely. The evidence indicates however that such attempts are likely to prove fruitless. This is because it is a mistake to believe that it is only prejudiced people who categorize and tolerant people who differentiate. The formulation and the use of prior assumptions is natural – what causes difficulties is the content of such assumptions (Eiser, 1990). Therefore, while the absolute elimination of stereotyping is almost certainly impossible what can be done is to find ways to modify stereotypes in order to reduce 'the harmful or unacceptable extremes of derogatory stereotypes and discriminatory behaviour' (Hogg and Abrams, 1988, p. 85). In other words, efforts should be concentrated on altering the content of stereotypes instead of trying to end stereotyping entirely.

It is easy to criticize the absence of good research in the area of children and peace. However, in mitigation it has to be remembered that until recently most psychological efforts at understanding conflict and attaining peace were concentrated on the problem of international wars, in particular on the global threat of nuclear war. Today, the world is no longer threatened to the same extent by conventional warfare but by ethnic conflicts, many of them internal. Researchers need to take this into account in planning future research.

One area in which promising work has already begun, as noted in chapter 5, concerns the concept of patriotism. At one level patriotism can be understood in terms of Social Identity Theory, as an example of in-group identification and the search for a positive self-concept (Schatz, 1993). However, as Schatz (1993) also points out, patriotism is particularly important because it is intrinsically linked to countries and countries are groups which differ from other groups in at least two important ways – first they control resources such as food and energy and secondly they almost always control a military force. This means that patriotism 'is an extraordinarily powerful phenomenon because the interests of the individual coincide with the political interests of the state' (Schatz, 1993, p. 28).

Despite this, patriotism is thought to be something positive into which most of the world's children are socialized. It is tempting, therefore, to suggest that somehow patriotism should be eliminated. According to Cohen and Arone (1988) not only would this be difficult to do, but it would be a mistake. They make the point that peace makers must learn that for groups in conflict 'identity precedes peace as a basic value'. Their answer is to see patriotism (they use the term nationalism) as 'the raw material' from which to fashion a solution to conflict by finding a way to substitute peace for war, while at the same time enhancing national pride and identity. Obviously these are ideas which are at a very early stage of development but which deserve much closer scrutiny.

Also more attention must be given to children's ideas about the future. This could be a particularly fruitful area if it is true (Boulding, 1988) that 'being able to picture a desired future is empowering' and that this is especially true where there is the capacity to create images of a wholly different future. Certainly Raundalen and Dodge (1991) based on their field experiences in the Third World claim that 'many children invest their entire hope for the future in whether their nation can cope'. If their assessment of the situation is correct this again may be an example of how identification with a group can mean that children's 'concerns become political instead of personal' (Raundalen and Dodge, 1991).

Action Research

In order to help bring about world peace psychologists, especially western psychologists, will have to consider the possibility of becoming accelerators or even initiators of social change if they really want to become concerned with prevention as much as with relief (Armenian, 1989; Moghaddam, 1990).

One way in which psychologists can fill this role is by becoming involved in 'action research'. Action research is field research in which the researcher is an active element in the actual project and in which the researcher becomes an 'independent variable in the research process' (Roe, 1993b, p. 6). This is not as straightforward as it sounds however. In particular, there are likely to be two main problems for western researchers, first in the way that they will be received by the people in the society they choose to help, and secondly in the way in which they will be judged by their fellow psychologists.

The first problem centres on the fact that if psychologists become involved as instigators of social change this will inevitably result in their being perceived as having explicit political aims. This in turn will mean that they will run the risk of being opposed by ruling power groups (Moghaddam, 1990).

The second problem is that in the academic world, as the history of the peace psychology movement illustrates, there is a belief, often unspoken, that 'relevant' research is inevitably less rigorous. This is of course a false dichotomy. Relevant research is only different because it is not neutral.

Nevertheless, one must not underestimate the challenges and difficulties that these issues present. In particular there is always the danger that researchers will adopt the role of activist to the detriment of the role of psychologist.

Fervent advocacy of any cause can influence the scientist's openness about the limitations of data relevant to a debate, can indeed increase the temptation to consider only evidence which strengthens one's own position and, worst of all, can even lead scientists to suppress data which support the 'other' side. To avoid these problems, as Hickson and Kriegler (1991) point out, it is important to strike a balance between functioning as an agent for change within a societal framework, while still maintaining a professional identity.

One benefit from adopting an action research perspective is that this should ensure that researchers do not fall into the trap of decontextualizing their research as noted earlier.

Influencing Policy

Psychologists could also further the cause of children and peace by trying to influence policy. However, becoming involved in policy-making is often a difficult step for psychologists to take because of the absence of any such tradition in their discipline. One problem is deciding just when there is enough data even to try to influence policy. On the other hand, what psychologists have to appreciate is that if they do not become involved others will take their place.

Also, even if psychologists do decide to get involved in influencing policy decisions they still face certain problems in translating 'research data into prescription' (Liddell and Kvalsvig, 1990). For example, it has been suggested that there may be an inherent bias in a lot of psychological research which hampers its usefulness in the policy arena. This is because in traditional research designs experimental treatments are meant to be as different from each other as possible. However, as Suedfeld and Tetlock (1992) point out in the real world a politically acceptable solution often calls for integrative policy mixes.

Yet another criticism of conventional, that is western, psychology is that it is based largely on what Moghaddam (1990) has called modulative psychology. This is psychology which has not been concerned directly with macrosocial processes, such as large-scale social and economic changes, but rather with the consequences of such changes. One reason for this (Suedfeld and Tetlock, 1992) is that at the macro-level problems become too complicated for research psychologists who tend to employ what are essentially laboratory-based designs. As a result there has been a concentration on more micro-level problems with the result that western psychology has tended to act as a force for stability in Third World settings (Moghaddam, 1990; Roe, 1993b).

Conclusions

This book has shown, that despite the well-meaning activities in the past, of a small number of psychologists, the quest to understand the repercussions of children's exposure to political violence has only made limited progress. Because of the disparate nature of the literature a basic problem has been that researchers have not always been aware of what has already been achieved. Hopefully this book will go some way to remedying that situation.

What this literature reveals is that there has been too much emphasis on the area of stress and coping and much less attention played to other equally important but less obvious topics, such as the impact of political violence on levels of aggression, moral development, and political socialization.

Unfortunately, as this book has also shown, the existing research has suffered from notable weaknesses which have hampered general progress in understanding how children react to political violence, as well as delaying any contribution to a search for peace.

Apart from basic problems related to design and measurement, perhaps the most significant weakness is that the research has tended to have been too narrow in scope. In particular there has been too close a focus on individuals rather than on groups or communities. This stems from various problems with western psychology which, for example, has been inclined to regard individualism and collectivism as opposite tendencies. This has presented a particular problem when thinking about children and political violence, because a critical feature of political violence is that it is a context in which 'individualism and collectivism are not mutually exclusive' (Punamaki, 1988, p. 6).

This tendency to adopt a decontextualized approach with no acknowledgement of socio-political factors is in turn related to another major weakness. This is the failure to recognize the importance of other academic disciplines, for example, economics and politics, and the resultant lack of collaboration with researchers from these disciplines.

In part, these problems stem from the 'scientific' method adopted by most psychologists in the west which has worked better at the micro rather than the macro-level. As a result virtually none of the psychological research in this area has had an impact on policy. One suggestion to overcome some if not all of these problems is to adopt a greater emphasis on action research.

Finally, it was argued that too much of existing research has been atheoretical. What this book has suggested is that Social Identity Theory can contribute to the development of research and understanding on such basic issues as the causes of intergroup conflict and political violence, as well as making a contribution to the better understanding of related topics, such as coping with stress, moral development, and political socialization, and most importantly to understanding the largely unexplored interrelationship between these topics.

This brings me to my final point. This is not an easy area to work in. Often there are personal dangers for researchers as well as professional problems. There are methodological problems in this area, which mean that researchers may have to be content with less than perfect designs and less than perfect data. Despite all these difficulties more research is needed, not just because this is an area which is badly under-researched, but because this work is important for the well-being of millions of children both in the short term and in the long term, by contributing to a search for global peace.

References

Acuna, J. E. (1988) *Children of the Storm: Experiences of the Children's Rehabilitation Centre.* Philippines: Children's Rehabilitation Centre.

Adam, H. (1990) Comparing Israel and South Africa. In P. L. van den Berghe (ed.), *State Violence and Ethnicity.* Nwiot, Colorado: University of Colorado Press.

Allodi, F. (1989) The children of victims of political persecution and torture: A psychological study of a Latin American refugee community. *International Journal of Mental Health*, 18, 2, 3–15.

Almond, G. A. (1960) A functional approach to comparative politics. In G. A. Almond and J. S. Coleman (eds), *The Politics of Developing Areas.* Princeton: Princeton University Press.

Amir, Y. (1969) Contact hypothesis in ethnic relations. *Psychological Bulletin*, 71, 319–42.

Anthony, E. J. (1986) Children's reactions to severe stress: The response to overwhelming stress: Some introductory comments. *Journal of the American Academy of Child Psychiatry*, 25, 3, 299–305.

Armenian, H. K. Perceptions from epidemiological research in an endemic war. *Social Science and Medicine*, 1989, 28, 7, 643–7.

Arroyo, W. and Eth, S. (1985) Children traumatized in Central American warfare. In S. Eth and R. S. Pynoos (eds), *Post-traumatic Stress Disorder in Children.* Washington, D.C.: American Psychiatric Press.

Arthur, P. (1974) *The People's Democracy 1968–73.* Belfast: Black-staff Press.

Assal, A. and Farrell, E. (1992) Attempts to make meaning of terror. *Anthropology and Education Quarterly*, 23, 4, 275–90.

Ayalon, O. (1983) Coping with terrorism. In D. Meichenbaum and M. Jaremko (eds), *Stress Reduction and Prevention*. New York: Plenum.

Bandura, A. (1990) Mechanisms of moral disengagement. In W. Reich (ed.), *Origins of Terrorism: Psychologies, Ideologies, Theologies, States of Mind*. New York: Cambridge University Press

Barner-Barry, C. and Rosenwein, R. (1985) *Psychological Perspectives on Politics*. Englewoods Cliffs, NJ: Prentice Hall.

Bat-Zion, N. and Levy-Shiff, R. (1993) Children in war: stress and coping reactions under the threat of scud missile attacks and the effect of proximity. In L. Leavitt and N. Fox (eds), *The Psychological Effects of War and Violence on Children*. Hillsdale, NJ: Lawerence Erlbaum.

Ben-Ari, R. and Amir, Y. (1988) Intergroup contact, cultural information and change in ethnic attitudes. In W. Stroebe, A. W. Kruglanski, D. Bat-Tal and M. Hewstone, *The Social Psychology of Intergroup Conflict: Theory, Research and Applications*. London: Springer-Verlag.

Bender, L. and Frosch, J. (1942) Children's reactions to the war. *American Journal of Orthopsychiatry*, 22, 571–86.

Berkowitz, L. (1990) On the formation and regulation of anger and angry aggression: a cognitive-neoassociationist analysis. *American Psychologist*, 45, 494–503.

Black D., Kaplan, T. and Harris, J. (1993) Father kills mother: effects on the children in the United Kingdom. In J. P. Wilson and B. Raphael (eds), *International Handbook of Traumatic Stress Syndromes*. New York: Plenum.

Bodman, F. (1941) War conditions and the mental health of the child. *British Medical Journal*, 2, 486–8.

Bodman, F. (1944) Child psychiatry in war-time Britain. *Journal of Educational Psychology*, 35, 5 (May), 293–301.

Bodman, F. H. and Dunsdon, M. I. (1941) Juvenile delinquency in war-time: report from the Bristol child-guidance clinic. *The Lancet*, November, 572–4.

Boothby, N. (1990) Working in the war zone. A look at psychological theory and practice from the field. *Mind and Human Interaction*, 2, 2, 30–36.

Boulding, E. (1988) Image and action in peace building. *Journal of Social Issues*, 44, 2, 17–37.

Bowlby, J. (1940) Psychological aspects. In R. Padley and M. Cole, *Evacuation Survey: A Report to the Fabian Society.* London: George Routledge and Sons Ltd.

Boyle, K., Chesney, R. and Hadden T. (1976) Who are the terrorists? *New Society*, 6 May, 299.

Breslin, A. Tolerance and moral reasoning among adolescents in Ireland. *Journal of Moral Education*, 1982, ii, 2, 112–27.

Breznitz, S. (ed.) (1983) *The Denial of Stress.* New York: International Universities Press.

Bronfenbrenner, U. (1962) The role of age, sex, class and culture in studies of moral development. *Religious Education*, 57, 4, 3–17

Brown, R. (1988) *Group Processes: Dynamics Within and Between Groups.* Oxford: Basil Blackwell.

Bryce, J., Walker, N., Ghorayeb, F. and Kanj, M. (1989) Life experiences, response styles and mental health among mothers and children in Beirut, Lebanon. *Social Science and Medicine*, 28, 7, 685–95.

Bryce, J. W. (1986) *Cries of Children in Lebanon.* Amman, Jordan: UNICEF

Bryce, J. W., Walker, N. and Peterson, C. (1989) Predicting symptoms of depression among women in Beirut: the importance of daily life. *International Journal of Mental Health*, 18, 1, 57–70.

Burman, S. (1986) The contexts of childhood in South Africa. In S. Burman and P. Reynolds (eds), *Growing Up in a Divided Society: Contexts of Childhood in South Africa.* Johannesburg: Raven Press.

Burt, C. (1942) The incidence of neurotic symptoms among evacuated children. *British Journal of Educational Psychology*, 10, 8–15.

Burt, C. and Simmins, C. A. (1942) Review of 'the Cambridge evacuation survey' *British Journal of Educational Psychology*, 7, 71–5.

Burton, F. (1979) *The Politics of Legitimacy.* London: Routledge.

Cairns, E. (1980) The development of ethnic discrimination in young children in Northern Ireland. In J. Harbison and J. Harbison (eds), *A Society under Stress: Children and Young People in Northern Ireland.* London: Open Books.

Cairns, E. (1982) Intergroup conflict in Northern Ireland. In H. Tajfel (ed.), *Social Identity and Intergroup Relations.* Cambridge: Cambridge University Press.

Cairns, E. (1983) Children's perceptions of normative and prescriptive interpersonal aggression in high and low areas of violence in

Northern Ireland. Unpublished paper. Coleraine: University of Ulster.

Cairns, E. (1984) Television news as a source of knowledge about the violence for children in Ireland: a test of the knowledge gap hypothesis. *Current Psychological Research and Reviews* (Winter), 32–8.

Cairns, E. (1987) *Caught in Crossfire: Children and the Northern Ireland Conflict*. Belfast and New York: Appletree Press and Syracuse University Press.

Cairns, E. (1990) Impact of television news exposure on children's perceptions of violence in Northern Ireland. *Journal of Social Psychology*, 130, 4, 447–52.

Cairns, E. (1992) Society as child abuser: Northern Ireland. In W. Stainton Rogers, D. Hevey and E. Ash (eds), *Child Abuse and Neglect: Facing the Challenge*. London: Batsford and The Open University.

Cairns, E., and Cairns, T. (1995). Children and Conflict: A Psychological Perspective. In S. Dunn (ed.) *Facets of the Conflict in Northern Ireland*. New York: St. Martin's Press.

Cairns, E. and Conlon, L. (1985) Children's moral reasoning and the Northern Irish violence. Unpublished paper. Coleraine: University of Ulster.

Cairns, E. and Wilson, R. (1993) Stress, coping and political violence in Northern Ireland. In J. P. Wilson and B. Raphael (eds), *International Handbook of Traumatic Stress Syndromes*. New York: Plenum Press.

Caul, B. (1983) Juvenile offender in Northern Ireland – a statistical review. In B. Caul, J. Pinkerton and F. Powell (eds), *The Juvenile Justice system in Northern Ireland*. Belfast: University of Ulster.

Chikane, F. (1986) Children in turmoil: the effects of the unrest on township children. In S. Burman and P. Reynolds (eds), *Growing Up in a Divided Society: Contexts of Childhood in South Africa*. Johannesburg: Raven Press.

Chimienti, G. and Nasr J. (1993) Children's reactions to war-related stress II. The influence of gender, age, and the mother's reaction. *International Journal of Mental Health*, 21, 4, 72–86.

Chimienti, G., Nasr, J. and Khalifehi, L. (1989) Children's reactions to war-related stress-affective symptoms and behaviour problems. *Social Psychiatry and Psychiatric Epidemiology*, 24, 6, 282–7.

Clark, R. P. (1986) Patterns in the lives of ETA members. In P. Merkle, (ed.), *Political Violence and Terror*. Berkeley and Los Angeles: University of California Press.

Cobb, S. (1976) Social support as a mediator of life stress. *Psychosomatic Medicine*, 38, 300–14.

Cohen, S. P. and Arone, H. C. (1988) Conflict resolution as the alternative to terrorism. *Journal of Social Issues*, 44, 2, 175–89.

Coles, R. (1986) *The Political Life of Children*. Boston: Houghton Mifflin Co.

Comite de Defensa de los Derechos del Pueblo (1989), The effects of torture and political repression in a sample of Chilean families. *Social Science and Medicine*, 28, 7, 735–40.

Committee on Labour and Human Resources, United States Senate (1990). Hearing before the United States Congressional Subcommittee on Children, Family Drugs and Alcoholism: Examining the effects of war and dislocation upon children. Washington: U.S. Government Printing Office.

Coogan T. P. (1987) *The IRA*. London: Fontana.

Cook, T. E. (1985) The bear market in political socialization and the cost of misunderstood psychological theories. *The American Political Science Review*, 79, 1079–93.

Cook, T. E. (1989) The Psychological theory of political-socialization and the political theory of child development – the dangers of normal science. *Human Development*, 32, 1, 24–34

Cooper, P. (1965) The development of the concept of war. *Journal of Peace Research*, 2, 1, 1–17.

Cortabile, A., Genta, M. L., Zuchinni, A., Smith, P. K., Harker, R. (1992) Attitudes of parents towards war play in young children. *Early Education and Development*, 3, 4, 356–69.

Crenshaw, M. (1990) Questions to be answered, research to be done, knowledge to be applied. In W. Reich (ed.), *Origins of Terrorism: Psychologies, Ideologies, Theologies, States of Mind*. New York: Cambridge University Press

Crichton-Miller, H. (1941) Somatic factors conditioning air-raid reactions. *The Lancet,* July 12, 31–34.

Crosby, T. L. (1986) *The Impact of Civilian Evacuation in the Second World War*. London: Croom Helm.

Curran, D. (1984) Juvenile offending, civil disturbance and political terrorism – a psychological perspective. Unpublished Paper. Belfast: University of Ulster.

Daly, B. and Vaughan, J. (1988) *Children at War*. London: Macdonald

Daly, C. (1989) Address to the Conference of the Council for Catholic Maintained Schools. Newcastle, N. Ireland: October.

Danziger, K. (1963a) The psychological future of an oppressed group. *Social Forces*, 42, 31–40.

Danziger, K. (1963b) Ideology and utopia in South Africa: a methodological contribution to the sociology of knowledge. *British Journal of Sociology* 14, 59–76.

Darweish, M. (1989) The intifada: social change. *Race and Class*, 31, 2, 47–61.

Dawes, A. (1990) The effects of political violence on children: a consideration of South African and related studies. *International Journal of Psychology*, 25, 1, 13–31.

Dawes, A. (1992) Political and moral learning in contexts of political conflict. Paper presented to the conference The Mental Health of Refugee Children Exposed to Violent Environments, Oxford.

Dawes, A. (1994a) The emotional impact of political violence. In A. Dawes and D. Donald (eds), *Childhood and Adversity: Psychological Perspectives from South African Research*. Cape Town: David Philip.

Dawes, A. (1994b) The effects of political violence on socio-moral reasoning and conduct. In A. Dawes and D. Donald (eds), *Childhood and Adversity: Psychological Perspectives from South African Research*. Cape Town: David Philip.

Dawes, A. and Donald, D. (1994) Understanding the psychological consequences of adversity. In A. Dawes and D. Donald (eds), *Childhood and Adversity: Psychological Perspectives from South African Research*. Cape Town: David Philip.

Dawes, A. and Tredoux, C. (1989) Emotional states of children exposed to political violence in the Crossroads squatter area during 1987/1988. *Psychology and Society*, 12, 33–47.

Dawes, A., Tredoux, C. and Feinstein, A. (1989) Political violence in South Africa: some effects on children of the violent destruction of their community. *International Journal of Mental Health*, 18, 2, 16–43

Derforges, D. M., Lord, C. G., Ramsey, S. L., Mason, J. A., van Loeuwen, M. D. and West, S. C. (1991) Effects of structured cooperative contact on changing negative attitudes toward stigmatized social groups. *Journal of Personality and Social Psychology*, 60, 4, 531–544.

Despert, J. L. (1942) *Preliminary Report on Children's Reactions to the War*. New York Hospital and Department of Psychiatry, Cornell University.

Deutch, M. (1990) Psychological roots of moral exclusion. *Journal of Social Issues*, 46, 1, 21–5.

Devlin, B. (1969) *The Price of My Soul*. London: André Deutsch.

Dijker, A. J. M. (1987) Emotional reactions to ethnic minorities. *European Journal of Social Psychology*, 17, 305–25.

Dodge, C. P. (1990) Health implications of war in Uganda and Sudan. *Social Sciences and Medicine*, 31, 6, 691–8.

Dodge, C. P. (1991) National and societal implications of war on children. In C. P. Dodge and M. Raundalen (eds), *Reaching Children in War: Sudan, Uganda and Mozambique*. Bergen, Norway: Sigma Forlag.

Dreman, S. (1989) Children of victims of terrorism in Israel – coping and adjustment in the face of trauma. *Israel Journal of Psychiatry and Related Sciences*, 26, 4, 212–22

Dudson, M. I. (1941) A psychologist's contribution to air-raid problems. *Mental Health*, 2, 37–41.

Dunn, S. (1993) Conflict, Reconstruction and Education. Paper presented on the occasion of the visit to Northern Ireland of the National commission on Education, Queen's University Belfast.

Dwork, D. (1991) *Children with a Star: Jewish Youth in Nazi Europe*. New Haven: Yale University Press.

Dyregrov, A. and Raundalen, M. (1987) Children and the stress of war – a review of the literature. In P. Cole, C. P. Dodge and M. Raundalen (eds), *War, Violence and Children in Uganda*, ch. 4. Oxford: Oxford University Press.

Eberly, R. E. and Engdahl, B. E. (1991) Prevalence of somatic and psychiatric disorders among former prisoners of war. *Hospital and Community Psychiatry*, 42 (August), 8, 807–13.

Eiser, R. (1990) *Social Judgement*. Milton Keynes: Open University.

Eitinger, L. (1980) The concentration camp syndrome and its late sequelae. In J. E. Dimsdale (ed.), *Survivors, Victims and Perpetrators*. Washington, D.C.: Hemisphere (cited by Last (1988)).

Eitinger, L. and Strom, A. (1981) New investigations on the morality and morbidity of Norwegian ex-concentration camp prisoners. *Israeli Journal of Psychiatry and Related Sciences*, 18, 3, 173–94.

Elder, G. H. and Meguro, Y. (1987) Wartime in men's lives: a comparative study of American and Japanese cohorts. *International Journal of Behavioral Development*, 10, 4, 439–66.

Elliott, R. and Lockhart, W. H. (1980) Characteristics of scheduled offenders and juvenile delinquents. In J. Harbison and J. Harbison (eds), *A Society Under Stress: Children and Young People in Northern Ireland*. Shepton Mallet: Open books.

Emler, N. P. (1984) Differential involvement in delinquency: toward an interpretation in terms of reputation management. In B. A. Maher and W. B. Maher (eds) *Progress in Experimental Personality Research*, vol. 13, New York: Academic Press.

Engestrom, Y. (1988) The cultural-historical theory of activity and the study of political repression. *International Journal of Mental Health*, 17, 4, 29–41.

Erikson, E. (1950/1964) *Childhood and Society*. New York: Norton.

Erikson, E. (1980) *Identity and the Life Cycle*. New York: Norton.

Eth, S. (1990) Innocent victims in a violent world. *1989 Medical and Health Annual*, 316–22. Chicago: Encyclopaedia Britannica Inc.

Fanon, F. (1967) *The Wretched of the Earth*. Harmondsworth: Penguin Books.

Farver, J. A. and Frosch, D. L. (1996) L.A. Stories: Aggression in 'preschoolers' spontaneous narratives after the riots of 1992. *Child Development*.

Fee, F. (1980) Responses to a behavioural questionnaire of a group of Belfast children. In J. Harbison and J. Harbison (eds), *A Society Under Stress: Children and Young People in Northern Ireland*. Somerset: Open Books.

Fee, F. (1983) Educational change in Belfast school children 1975–81. In J. Harbison (ed.), *Children of the Troubles: Children in Northern Ireland*. Belfast: Stranmillis College Learning Resources Unit.

Feshbach, S. (1990) Psychology of human violence and the search for peace. *Journal of Social Issues*, 46, 1, 183–98.

Fields, R. M. (1973) *A Society on the Run: A Psychology of Northern Ireland*. Harmondsworth: Penguin.

Fields, R. M. (1977) *Society Under Siege: A Psychology of Northern Ireland*. Philadelphia: Temple University Press.

Figley, C. R. (1993) War-related stress and family-centred intervention: American children and the Gulf War. In L. Leavitt and N. Fox (eds), *The Psychological Effects of War and Violence on Children*. Hillsdale, NJ: Lawerence Erlbaum.

Finchilescu, G. and Dawes, A. (1993) Adolescents perspectives on social change in South Africa. Paper presented to the 11th Annual Congress of the Psychological Association of South Africa, September.

Folkman, S. and Lazarus, R. S. (1988) The relationship between coping and emotion: implications for theory and research. *Social Science and Medicine*, 26, 3, 309–17.

Foster, D. (1986) The development of racial orientation in children: a review of South African research. In S. Burman and P. Reynolds (eds), *Growing Up in a Divided Society: Contexts of Childhood in South Africa*. Johannesburg: Raven Press.

Foster, D. (1989). Political detention in South Africa: a sociopsychological perspective. *International Journal of Mental Health*, 18, 1, 21–37.

Foster, D. (1991) On racism: virulent mythologies and fragile threads. Inaugural Lecture, University of Cape Town.

Foster, D. and Finchilescu, G. (1986) Contact in a non-contact society: the case of South Africa. In M. Hewstone and R. Brown (eds), *Contact and Conflict in Intergroup Encounters*. Oxford: Basil Blackwell.

Foster, D. and Louw-Potgieter, J. (1991) *Social Psychology in South Africa*. Johannesburg: Lexicon.

Fraser, M. (1974) *Children in Conflict*. Harmondsworth: Penguin Books.

Freud, A. and Burlingham, D. T. (1943) *War and Children*. New York: International Universities Press.

Freud, A. and Dann, S. (1951) An experiment in group upbringing. In *The Psychoanalytic Study of the Child*, vol. 6. New York: International Universities Press.

Gaertner, S. L., Mann, J. A., Dovidio, J. F., Murrel, A. J. and Pomare, M. (1990) How does cooperation reduce intergroup bias. *Journal of Personality and Social Psychology*, 59, 4, 692–704.

Gallagher, A. M. (1992) Education in a divided society. *The Psychologist*, 5, 353–6.

Garbarino, J. and Bronfenbrenner, U. (1976) The socialization of moral judgement and behavior in cross-cultural perspective. In T. Lickona (ed.), *Moral Development and Behaviour: Theory, Research and Social Issues*. New York: Holt, Rinehart and Winston.

Garbarino, J. and Kostelny, K. (1993) Children's response to war: what do de know? In L. Leavitt and N. Fox (eds), *The Psychological Effects of War and Violence on Children*. Hillsdale, NJ: Lawerence Erlbaum.

Garbarino, J. and Kostelny, K. (1996) The effects of political violence on Palestinian Children's behaviour problems: A risk accumulation model. *Child Development*.

Garbarino, J., Kostelny, K. and Dubrow, N. (1991a) *No Place to be a Child*. New York: Lexington Books.

Garbarino, J., Kostelny, K. and Dubrow, N. (1991b) What can children tell us about living in danger. *American Psychologist*, 46 (April), 4, 376–83.

Garmezy, N. (1983) Stressors of childhood. In N. Garmezy and M. Rutter (eds), *Stress, Coping and Development in Children*. New York: McGraw-Hill.

Geddie, L. and Hildreth, G. (1944) Children's ideas about the war. *Journal of Experimental Education*, 12, 92–7.

Geiger, H. (1968) *The Family in Soviet Russia*. Cambridge Mass.: Harvard University Press.

Gibson, K. (1987) Civil conflict, stress and children. *Psychology in Society*, 8, 4.

Gibson, K. (1989) Children in political violence. *Social Science and Medicine*, 28, 7, 659–67.

Gibson, K. (1991) Indirect forms of political violence and their psychological effects on children in South Africa. Paper presented to the 3rd International Conference of Centres, Institutions and Individuals Concerned with the Care for Victims of Organized Violence: Health, Political Repression and Human Rights. Santagio, Chile.

Gillespie, J. M. and Allport, G. M. (1955) *Youth's Outlook on the Future: A Cross-national Study*. New York: Doubleday.

Gillespie, R. D. (1944) *Psychological Effects of War on Citizen and Soldier*. London: Chapman and Hall.

Graham, H. D. and Gurr, T. (1969) *The History of Violence in America*. New York: Praeger.

Greenstein, F. (1965) *Children and Politics*. New York: Yale University Press.

Greenstein, F. (1969) Queen and Prime Minister – the child's eye view. *New Society*, 14, 369, 635–8.

Grudzinkas-Gross (1981) *War Through Children's Eyes: The Soviet Occupation of Poland and the Deportations, 1939–1941*. Stanford University: Hoover Institution Press.

Hakvoort, I. and Oppenheimer, L. (1993) Children and adolescents conceptions of peace, war and strategies to attain peace – a Dutch case-study. *Journal of Peace Research*, 30, 1, 65–77.

Hareven, T. K. (1986) Historical changes in the family and the life course: Implications for child development. In A. Smuts and H. Hagen (eds) History and Research in Child Development. *Monographs of the Society for Research in Child Development*, 50, 4–5, serial No. 211.

Harris, R. (1989) Anthropological views on violence in Northern Ireland. In Y. Alexander and A. O'Day (eds), *Ireland's Terrorist Trauma: Interdisciplinary Perspectives*. New York: Harvester Weatsheaf.

Harrison, T. (1941) Obscure nervous effects of air raids. *British Medical Journal*, 2, 573–4.

Heskin, K. (1980a) Children and young people in Northern Ireland: a research review. In, J. Harbison and J. Harbison (eds), *A Society Under Stress: Children and Young People in Northern Ireland*. Shepton Mallet: Open Books.

Heskin, K. (1980b) *Northern Ireland: A Psychological Analysis*. Dublin: Gill and Macmillan.

Heskin, K. (1981) Societal disintegration in Northern Ireland: fact or fiction. *The Economic and Social Review*, 12, 2, 97–113.

Hewstone, M. and Brown, R (1986) *Contact and Conflict in Intergroup Encounters*. Oxford: Basil Blackwell.

Hickson, J and Kriegler, S. (1991) The mission and role of psychology in a traumatised and changing society: the case of South Africa. *International Journal of Psychology*, 26, 783–793.

Hierholyer, R., Munzon, J., Peabody, C., Rosenberg, J. (1992) Clinical presentations of PTSD in World War II combat veterans. *Hospital and Community Psychiatry*, August, 43, 8, 817–822

Hoffmann, W. and McKenrdick, B. W. (1990) The nature of violence. In B. W. McKendrick and W. Hoffmann (eds), *People and Violence in South Africa*. Cape Town: Oxford University Press.

Hogg, M. A. (1992) *The Social Psychology of Group Cohesiveness: From Attraction to Social Identity*. New York: Harvester Wheatsheaf.

Hogg, M. A. and Abrams, D. (1988) *Social Identifications: A Social Psychology of Intergroup Relations and Group Processes*. London: Routledge.

Horowitz, E. L. (1936) Development of attitudes towards negroes. *Archives of Psychology*, no. 194.

Horowitz, E. L. (1940) Some aspects of the development of patriotism in children. *Sociometry*, 3, 329–41.

Horowitz, M. J. (1993) Stress response syndromes: a review of post traumatic stress and adjustment disorders. In J. P. Wilson and B. Raphael (eds), *International Handbook of Traumatic Stress Syndromes*. New York: Plenum.

Hosin, A. and Cairns, E. (1984) The impact of conflict on children's ideas about their country. *Journal of Psychology*, 118, 161–8.

Hovens, J. E., Falger, P. R., Op den Velde, W., Schouten, E. G. W., de Groen, J. H. M. and van Duijn, H. (1992) Occurrence of current post traumatic stress disorder among Dutch World War II resistance veterans according to the SCID. *Journal of Anxiety Disorder*, 6, 2, 147–57.

Hyman, H. (1959) *Political Socialization*. New York: Free Press.

Ingleby, D. (1988) Critical psychology in relation to political repression and violence. *International Journal of Mental Health*, 17, 4, 16–28.

International Child Welfare Review (1947) The War and Juvenile Delinquency. *International Child Welfare Review*, vol. 1, no. 2–3.

Jacobs, J. B. (1988) Families facing the nuclear taboo. *Family Relations*, 37, 432–6.

Jahoda, G. (1963) The development of children's ideas about country and nationality. I: the conceptual framework. *British Journal of Educational Psychology*, 33, 142–53.

Jensen, P. S. and Shaw, J. (1993) Children as victims of war: current knowledge and future research needs. *Journal of the American Academy of Child and Adolescent Psychiatry*, 32, 4, 697–708.

John, E. (1941) A study of the effects of evacuation and air-raids on pre-school children. *British Journal of Educational Psychology*, 11, 173–82.

Joseph, S. A., Brewin, C. R., Yule, W. and Williams, R. (1991) Causal attribution and psychiatric symptoms in survivors of the Herald of Free Enterprise disaster. *British Journal of Psychiatry*, 159, 542–6.

Kahn, J. V. (1982) Moral reasoning in Irish children and adolescents as measured by the Defining Issues Test. *Irish Journal of Psychology*, 2, 96–108.

Kimmins, C. W. (1915) The special interests of children in the war at different ages. *Journal of Experimental Pedagogy and Training College Record*, 3, 3, 145–52.

Kinzie, J. D., Sack, W. H., Angell, R. H., Manson, S. and Rath, B. (1986) The psychiatric effects of massive trauma on Cambodian children: I: The children. *Journal of the American Academy of Child Psychiatry*, 25, 370.

Klingman, A., Sagi, A. and Raviv, A. (1993) The effects of war on Israeli children. In L. Leavitt and N. Fox (eds), *The Psychological Effects of War and Violence on Children*. Hillsdale, NJ: Lawerence Erlbaum.

Knutson, J. (1981) Victimization as a root of political violence. Unpublished Paper. Los Angeles: University of California.

Kohlberg, L. (1984) *Essays on Moral development: The Psychology of Moral Development: The Nature and validity of Moral Stages*, 2. San Francisco: Harper and Row.

Krupinski, J. and Docent, M. D. (1967) Sociological aspects of mental ill-health in migrants. *Social Science and Medicine*, 1, 267–81.

Kuttab, D. (1988) A profile of the stone throwers. *Journal of Palestine Studies*, 17, 14–23.

Last, U. (1988) The transgenerational impact of Holocaust traumatization: current state of the evidence *International Journal of Mental Health*, 17, 4, 72–89.

Last, U. and Klein, H. (1984) Impact of parental Holocaust traumatization on offsprings' reports of parental child rearing practices. *Journal of Youth and Adolescence*, l3, 267–83.

Lazarus, R. S. and Folkman, S. (1984) *Stress, Appraisal and Coping*. New York: Springer.

Lederer, E. (1994) *Children at War*. Associated Press Release, December 11.

Leeson, C. (1917) *The Child and the War: Being Notes on Juvenile Delinquency*. London: The Howard Association.

Leon, G. R., Butcher, J. N., Kleinman, M., Goldberg, A. and M. Almagor (1981) Survivors of the Holocaust and their children: current status and adjustment. *Journal of Personality and Social Psychology*, 41, 503.

Lewis, A. (1942) Incidence of neurosis in England under war conditions. *Lancet*, 2 (15 August), 175–83.

Lickona, T. (1976) Critical issues in the study of moral development and behaviour. In. T. Lickona (ed.), *Moral Development and Behaviour: Theory, Research and Social Issues*. New York: Holt, Rinehart and Winston.

Liddell, C. and Kvalsvig, J. (1990) Science and accountability: issues related to South African developmental psychology. *South African Journal of Psychology*, 20, 1, 1–9

Liddell, C., Kemp, J. and Moema, M. (1993) The young lions – South African children and youth in political struggle. In L. Leavitt and N. Fox (eds), *The Psychological Effects of War and Violence on Children*. Hillsdale, NJ: Lawerence Erlbaum.

Liddell, C., Kvalsvig, J., Qotyana, P. and Shabalala, A. (1994) Community violence and young South African children's involvement in aggression. *International Journal of Behavioral Development*, 17, 4, 613–28.

Liddell, C., Kvalsvig, J., Shababala, A. and Masilela, P. (1991) Historical perspectives on South African childhood. *International Journal of Behavioral Development*, 14, 1, 1–19.

Linn, R. (1989) *Not Shooting and Not Crying: Psychological Inquiry into Moral Disobedience*. New York: Greenwood Press.

Lorenc, L. and Branthwaite, A. (1986) Evaluation of violence by English and Northern Ireland schoolchildren. *British Journal of Social Psychology*, 25, 4, 349–52.

Lyons, H. A. and Harbinson, H. J. (1986) A comparison of political and non-political murders in Northern Ireland, 1974–84. *Medical Scientific Law*, 26, 3, 193–7.

Lyons, H. A. (1987) Post-traumatic stress disorder in children and adolescents: a review of the literature. *Developmental and Behavioural Pediatrics*, 8, 6, 349–56.

McArdle, D. (1949) *Children of Europe. A study of the children of liberated countries: their war-time experiences, their reactions and their needs with a note on Germany*. London: Victor Gollancz.

McCauley, C. and Segal, M. E. (1987) Social psychology of terrorist groups. In C. Hendrick (ed.), *Group Processes and Intergroup Relations. Review of Personality and Social Psychology*, 9. London: Sage.

McCauley, P. and Kremer, J. M. D. (1990) On the fringes of society: adults and children in a West Belfast community. *New Community*, 16, 2, 247–59.

McFarlane, A. C., Policansky, S. K. and Irwin, C. (1987) A longitudinal study of the psychological morbidity in children due to natural disaster. *Psychological Medicine*, 17, 727–38.

McGhee, R., Williams, S., Bradshaw, J., Chapel, J. L., Robins, A. and Silva P. A. (1985) The Rutter Scale for completion by teachers: factor structure and relationships with cognitive abilities and family adversity for a sample of New Zealand children. *Journal of Child Psychology and Psychiatry*, 26, 727–39.

McGrath, A. and Wilson, R. (1985) Factors which influence the prevalence and variation of psychological problems in children in Northern Ireland. Paper presented to the Annual of the Developmental Section of the British Psychological Society, Belfast.

McKendrick, B. W. and Hoffmann, W. Towards the reduction of violence. In B. W. McKendrick and W. Hoffmann (eds), *Political Violence in South Africa* (1990). Cape Town: Oxford University Press.

McKernan, J. (1980) Pupil values as indicators of intergroup differences in Northern Ireland. In J. Harbison and J. Harbison (eds), *A Society Under Stress: Children And Young People In Northern Ireland*. London: Open Books.

Macksoud, M., Dyregrov, A. and Raundalen, M. (1993) Traumatic war experiences and their effects on children. In J. P. Wilson and B. Raphael (eds), *International Handbook of Traumatic Stress Syndromes*. New York: Plenum.

Mahjoub, A., Leyens, J. P., Yzerbvt, V. and Digiacomo, J. P. (1989) War stress and coping modes-representations of self-identity and time perspective among Palestinian children. *International Journal of Mental Health*, 1989, 18, 2, 44–62.

Majodina, Z. (1989) Exile as a chronic stressor. *International Journal of Mental Health*, 18, 1, 87–94.

Malmquist, C. (1986) Children who witness parental murder: post-traumatic aspects. *Journal of the American Academy of Child Psychiatry*, 25, 320–5.

Malteno, C., Kibel, M. and Roberts, M. (1986) Childhood health in South Africa. In S. Burman and P. Reynolds (eds), *Growing up in a Divided Society: The Contexts of Childhood in South Africa*.

Marcus-Newhall, A. and Miller, N. (1993) Cross-cutting category membership with role assignment. A means of reducing inter-group bias. *British Journal of Social Psychology*, 23, 32, 125–46.

McWhirter, L. (1983) How 'troubled' are children in Northern Ireland compared to children who live outside Northern Ireland? Paper presented to the Annual Conference of the Psychological Society of Ireland, Athlone.

McWhirter, L. (1988) Psychological impact of violence in Northern Ireland: recent research findings and issues. In N. Eisenberg and D. Glasgow (eds), *Recent Advances in Clinical Psychology*. London: Gower.

McWhirter, L. (1990) How do children cope with the chronic troubles of Northern Ireland. Paper presented to the Conference Children in War, Jerusalem.

McWhirter, L. (1981) Northern Irish children's conceptions of violent crime. *The Howard Journal*, 21, 167–77.

Meijer, A. (1985) Child psychiatric sequelae of maternal war stress. *Acta Psychiatrica Scandinavica*, 72, 505.

Mercer, G. W. and Bunting, B. (1980) Some motivations of adolescent demonstrators in the Northern Ireland civil disturbances. In J. Harbison and J. Harbison (eds), *A Society Under Stress: Children and Young People in Northern Ireland*. Open Books: Somerset.

Merkle, P. (ed.) (1986) *Political Violence and Terror*. Berkeley and Los Angeles: University of California Press.

Merkle, P. H. (1986) Conclusions: collective purposes and individual motives. In P. Merkle (ed.), *Political Violence and Terror*. Berkeley and Los Angeles: University of California Press.

Mi'ari, M. (1989) The effect of the uprising on readiness for interethnic contact among Palestinians in Israel. *International Journal of Comparative Sociology*, 30, 3–4, 238–46.

Milgram, N. A. (1982) War-related stress in Israeli children and youth. In L. Goldberger and S. Breznitz, *Handbook of Stress: Theoretical and Clinical Aspects*. New York: Free Press.

Milgram, N. A. (1993) War-related trauma and victimization: principles of traumatic stress prevention in Israel. In J. P. Wilson and B. Raphael (eds), *International Handbook of Traumatic Stress Syndromes*. New York: Plenum.

Milgram, R. M. and Milgram, N. A. (1976) The effect of the Yom Kippur War on anxiety level in Israeli children. *Journal of Psychology*, 94, 107–13.

Miller, E. (1940) *The Neuroses in War*. London: Macmillan.

Miller, G. (1969) Psychology as a means of promoting human welfare. *American Psychologist*, 24, 1063–1075.

Miller, K. E. (1996) The effects of state terrorism and exile in indigenous Guatemalan refugee children: A mental health assessment and an analysis of children's narratives. *Child Development*.

Moghaddam, F. M. (1990) Modulative and generative orientations in psychology: implications for psychology in the three worlds. *Journal of Social Issues*, 46, 3, 21–41.

Moscovici, S. (1990) Social psychology and developmental psychology: extending the conversation. In G. Duveen and B. Lloyd (eds), *Social Representations and the Development of Knowledge*. Cambridge: Cambridge University Press.

Murphy, H. B. M. (1984) Minority status, civil strife and the major disorders: hospitalization patterns in Northern Ireland. Unpublished paper.

Murray, H. A. Prospect for psychology. In G. S. Neilsen (ed.), *Psychology and International Affairs: Can we Contribute*. Copenhagen: Munksgaard.

Myers-Walls, J. A , Myers-Bowman, K. S. and Pelo. A. E. (1993) Parents as Educators about War and Peace, *Family Relations*, 42, 1, 66–73.

Nader, K. and Pynoos, S. (1993) The children of Kuwait after the Gulf crisis. In L. Leavitt and N. Fox (eds), *The Psychological Effects of War and Violence on Children*. Hillsdale, NJ: Lawrence Erlbaum.

Nadler, A., Kav-Venaki, S. and Gleitman, B. (1985) Transgenerational effects of the Holocaust. Externalization of aggression in second generation of Holocaust survivors. *Journal of Consulting and Clinical Psychology*, 53, 365–9.

Nasson, B. (1986) Perspectives on education in South Africa. In S. Burman and P. Reynolds (eds), *Growing Up in a Divided Society: Contexts of Childhood in South Africa*. Johannesburg: Raven Press.

National Advisory Commission on Civil Disorders (1968). New York: Bantam Books.

Nissan, M. and Koriat, A. (1989) Moral justification of acts judged to be morally right and acts judged to be morally wrong. *British Journal of Social Psychology*, 28, 3, 213–25.

Novello, A. C. (1991) Violence is a greater killer of children than disease. *Public Health Reports*, 106, 3, 231–3.

Palme, E. (1991) Personal reflections on the new rights for children in war. In C. P. Dodge and M. Raundalen (1991) *Reaching Children in War: Sudan, Uganda and Mozambique*. Bergen, Norway: Sigma Forlag.

Park, C., Cohen, L. H. and Herb, L. (1990) Intrinsic religiousness and religious coping as life stress moderators for Catholic versus Protestants. *Journal of Personality and Social Psychology*, 5, 3, 562–74.

Pettigrew, T. F. (1986) the intergroup contact hypothesis reconsidered. In M. Hewstone and R. Brown (eds), *Contact and Conflict in Intergroup Encounters*. Oxford: Basil Blackwell.

Piaget, J. (1934) Is an education for peace possible? *Bulletin de l'Enseignement de la Société des Nations*, 1, 17–23; translation by H. G. Furth in the *Genetic Epistemologist* (1987), 17, 3, 5–9.

Piaget, J. (1987) Is an education for peace possible? *The Genetic Epistemologist*, 17, 3, 5–9; translation by H. G. Furth from Bulletin de l'Enseignement de la Société des Nations, 1934, 1, 17–23).

Piaget, J. and Weil, A. M. (1951) The development in children of the idea of homeland, and of relations with other countries. *International Social Science Bulletin*, 3, 561–78.

Poole, M. (1983) The demography of violence. In J. Darby (ed.), *Northern Ireland: The Background to the Troubles*. Belfast: Appletree Press.

Post, J. M. (1990) Terrorist psycho-logic: terrorist behaviour as a product of psychological forces. In W. Reich (ed.), *Origins of*

Terrorism: Psychologies, Ideologies, Theologies, States of Mind. New York: Cambridge University Press.

Potter, J. and Wetherell, M. (1987) *Discourse and Social Psychology: Beyond Attitudes and Behaviour.* London: Sage.

Pritchard, R. and Rosenzweig, S. (1942) The effects of war stress upon childhood and youth. *The Journal of Abnormal and Social Psychology*, 37 (July), 3, 329–44.

Protacio-Marcelino, E. (1989) Children of political detainees in the Philippines: sources of stress and coping patterns. *International Journal of Mental Health*, 18, 1, 71–86.

Pryor, C. B. (1992) School's defence of children in America at war. *Urban Education*, 27, 1, 7–20.

Punamaki, R-L. (1987) Childhood under conflict: the attitudes and emotional life of Israeli and Palestinian children. Tampere: Tampere Peace Research Institute, Research Reports.

Punamaki, R-L. (1988) Political violence and mental health: some theoretical considerations regarding research. *International Journal of Mental Health*, 17, 4, 3–15.

Punamaki, R-L. (1989) Factors affecting the mental health of Palestinian children exposed to political violence. *International Journal of Mental Health*, 18, 2, 63–79.

Punamaki, R-L. (1993) The mental health function of play, dreaming and bereavement among children exposed to war experiences. Paper presented at the Third International Symposium on the Contributions of Psychology to Peace, Ashland, Virginia, August.

Punamaki, R-L. (1996) Can ideological commitment protect children's psychosocial well-being in situations of political violence? *Child Development.*

Punamaki, R-L. and Suleiman, R. (1990) Predictors and effectiveness of coping with political violence among Palestinian children. *British Journal of Social Psychology*, 29, 1, 67–77.

Pynoos, R. S. and Eths, S. (1985) Children traumatized by witnessing acts of personal violence. Homicide, rape, or suicidal behaviour. In S. Eth and R. S. Pynoos (eds), *Post-traumatic Stress Disorder in Children.* Washington, D.C.: American Psychiatric Press.

Pynoos, R. S. and Nader, K. (1989) Children's memory and proximity to violence. *Journal of the American Academy of Child and Adolescent Psychiatry*, 28, 2 , 236–41.

Rachman, S. J. (1990) *Fear and Courage.* San Francisco: W. H. Freeman.

Raundalen, M. and Dodge, C. P. (1991) Research challenges in practical perspective. In C. P. Dodge and M. Raundalen (1991) *Reaching Children in War: Sudan, Uganda and Mozambique.* Bergen, Norway: Sigma Forlag.

Raundalen, M., Lwanga, J. Mugisha, C. and Dyregov, A. (1987) Four investigations on stress among children in Uganda. In P. Cole, C. P. Dodge and M. Raundalen (eds), *War, Violence and Children in Uganda*, ch. 3. Oxford: Oxford University Press.

Rautman, A. L. and Brower, E. (1945) War themes in children's stories. *Journal of Psychology*, 25, 191–202.

Rautman, A. L. and Brower, E. (1951) War themes in children's stories: 6 years later. *Journal of Psychology*, 31, 263–70.

Reich, W. (1990) Understanding terrorist behaviour: the limits and opportunities of psychological inquiry. In W. Reich (ed.), *Origins of Terrorism: Psychologies, Ideologies, Theologies, States of Mind.* New York: Cambridge University Press.

Ress, Beber and Volker (1986) cited in Dawes (1992).

Ressler, E. M., Boothby, N. and Steinbock D. J. (1988) *Unaccompanied Children: Care and Protection in Wars, Natural Disasters, and Refugee Movements.* New York: Oxford University Press.

Reynolds, P. (1990) Children of tribulations: the need to heal and the means to heal war trauma. *Africa*, 60, 1, 1–38.

Richters, J. E. and Martinez, P. (1993) The NIMH community violence project: I Children as victims and witnesses to violence. *Psychiatry*, 56 (February), 7–21.

Roe, M. D. (1993a) Psychological and social resilience to political violence: role of faith communities. Paper presented to the 101st Annual Convention of the American Psychological Association. Toronto, Canada.

Roe, M. D. (1993b) Human responsibility and action scholarship: social scientists as advocates. In M. Madzkowski and A. Ellis (eds), *Humanitarian Values for Russian Secondary Schools*, 2. Moscow: International Centre for Human values.

Roe, M. D. (1994) Queries about protecting children in war settings. *The Peace Psychology Bulletin*, 3, 1, 12–18.

Roe, M. D. (in press) Psychosocial adaptation of Filipino evacuees in the Philippines. *National Social Science Journal.*

Rofe, Y. and Lewin, I. (1982) The effect of war environment on dreams and sleep habits. In N. A. Milgram (ed.), *Stress and Anxiety*, 8. New York: Hemisphere Publishing.

Ronstrom, A. (1989) Children in Central-America: victims of war. *Child Welfare*, 68, 2, 145–53.

Rose, S. L. and Garske, J. (1987) Family environment adjustment and coping among children of Holocaust survivors: a comparative investigation. *American Journal of Orthopsychiatry*, 57, 332.

Rosenblatt, R. (1983) *Children of War*. New York: Anchor Press/Doubleday.

Rutter, M. (1983) Stress, coping and development: some issues and some questions. In N. Garmezy and M. Rutter (eds), *Stress, Coping and Development in Children*. New York: McGraw-Hill.

Rutter, M., Cox, A., Tupling, C., Berger, M. and Yule, W. (1975) Attainment and adjustment in two geographical areas: 1 the prevalence of psychiatric disorders. *British Journal of Psychiatry*, 126, 520–33.

Sack, W. H., Angell, R. H., Kinzie, J. D. and Rath, B. (1986) The psychiatric effects of massive trauma on Cambodian children: II The family, the home, and the school. *Journal of the American Academy of Child Psychiatry*, 25, 377–83.

Sack, W. H., Clarke, G. N. and Secley, M. S. (1996) Mutiple forms of stress in Cambodian adolescent refugees. *Child Development*.

Schaffer D. R. (1989) *Developmental Psychology: Childhood and Adolescence* (2nd edn). Pacific Grove, Cal.: Brooks/Cole.

Schatz, R. T. (1993) Patriotism and intergroup conflict. *The Peace Psychology Bulletin*, 2, 3, 25–32.

Schwarzwald, J., Weisenberg, M., Waysman, M., Solomon, Z. and Klingman, A. (1993) Stress reaction of school-age children to the bombardment by SCUD missiles. *Journal of Abnormal Psychology*, 102, 3, 404–10.

Shanan, J. (1989) Surviving the survivors: late personality development of Jewish Holocaust survivors. *International Journal of Mental Health*, 17, 4, 42–71.

Sigal, J. J. (1973) Hypotheses and methodology in the study of families of the Holocaust survivors. In E. J. Anthony and C. Koupernik (eds), *The Child and his Family*, 2. New York: Wiley.

Sigal, J. J. and Weinfeld, M. (1985) Control of aggression in adult children of survivors of the nazi persecution. *Journal of Abnormal Psychology*, 94, 4, 556–64.

Silove, D. and Schweitzer, R. (1993) Apartheid: disastrous effects of a community in conflict. In J. P. Wilson and B. Raphael (eds), *International Handbook of Traumatic Stress Syndromes*. New York: Plenum.

Simpson, M. A. (1993) Bitter Waters: Effects on Children of the

Stresses of Unrest and Oppression. In J. P. Wilson and B. Raphael (eds), *International Handbook of Traumatic Stress Syndromes*. New York: Plenum.

Smith, M. C. and Zaidi, S. (1993) Malnutrition in Iraqi children following the Gulf War: results of a national survey. *Nutritional Reviews*, 51, 3, 74–8.

Smith, R. P. (1916) Proceeding of the Royal Society of Medicine, 10, Section Psychiat., (October), 1–20.

Sroufe, L. A. and Rutter, M. (1984) The domain of developmental psychology. *Child Development*, 55, 17–29.

Staub, E. (1989) *The Roots of Evil: The Origins of Genocide and other Group Violence*. New York: Cambridge University Press.

Stephan, W. G. and Brigham, J. C. (1985) Intergroup contact: introduction. *Journal of Social Issues*, 41, 3, 1–8.

Stephan, W. G. and Stephan, C. W. (1985) Intergroup anxiety. *Journal of Social Issues*, 41, 157–76.

Stewart, A. T. Q. (1977) *The Narrow Ground: Aspects of Ulster*. London: Faber and Faber.

Straker, G. (1990) Violence against children: emotional abuse. In B. W. McKendrick and W. Hoffmann (eds), *Political Violence in South Africa*. Cape Town: Oxford University Press.

Straker, G., Mendelsohn, M., Tudin, P. and Mooza, F. (1996) Violent political contexts and the emotional concerns of township youth. *Child Development*.

Suedfeld, P. and Tetlock, P. E. (1992) Psychologists as policy advocates: the roots of controversy. In P. Suedfeld and P. E. Tetlock (eds), *Psychology and Social Policy*. New York: Hemisphere Publishing.

Swartz, L. and Levett, A. (1989) Political repression and children in South Africa: the social construction of damaging effects. *Social Science and Medicine*, 28, 7, 741–50.

Tajfel, H. (1978) *Differentiation between Groups: Studies in the Social Psychology of Intergroup Relations*. London: Academic Press.

Tajfel, H. (1981) *Human Groups and Social Categories*. Cambridge: Cambridge University Press.

Taylor, M. (1988) *The Terrorist*. London: Brassey.

Taylor, R. (1989) *Families at War: Voices from the Troubles*. London: BBC Books.

Thomas, A. (1990) Violence and child detainees. In B. W. McKendrick and W. Hoffmann (eds), *Political Violence in South Africa*. Cape Town: Oxford University Press.

Thompson, J. L. P. (1986) Denial, polarization and genocidal massacre: a comparative analysis of Northern Ireland and Zanzibar. *Economic and Social Review*, 17, 4, 293–314.

Tiano, S. (1986) Authoritarianism and political culture in Argentina and Chile in the mid-1960's. *Latin American Research Review*, 21, 1, 73–98.

Titmus, R. M. (1950) *Problems of Social Policy*. London: His Majesty's Stationery Office.

Tolley, H. (1973) *Children and War*. New York: Teacher's College Press.

Trew, K. (1986) Catholic-Protestant contact in Northern Ireland. In M. Hewstone and R. Brown (eds), *Contact and Conflict in Intergroup Encounters*. Oxford: Basil Blackwell.

Turner, J. C. (1987) *Rediscovering the Social Group: A Self-Categorization Theory*. Oxford: Basil Blackwell.

UNICEF (1984) *The State of the World's Children 1985*. London: Oxford University Press.

Usher, G. (1991) Children of Palestine. *Race and Class*, 23, 4, 1–18.

Valentine, C. W. (1941) Editorial note on evacuation investigations. *British Journal of Educational Psychology*, 11, 127.

van den Berghe, P. L. (1990) *State Violence and Ethnicity*. Niwot, Colorado: University of Colorado Press.

van der Veer, G. Psychotherapy with young adult political refugees: a developmental approach. In J. P. Wilson and B. Raphael (eds), *International Handbook of Traumatic Stress Syndromes*. New York: Plenum.

van Ginneken, J. (1992) *Crowds, Psychology and Politics 1871–1899*. London: Cambridge University Press.

Vernon, P. E. (1941) Psychological effects of air-raids. *Journal of Abnormal and Social Psychology*, 36 (October), 4, 457–76.

Vikan, A. (1985) Psychiatric epidemiology in a sample of 1,510 ten-year-old children. *Journal of Child Psychology and Psychiatry*, 26, 55–75.

Waldmann, P. (1986) Guerrilla movements in Argentina, Guatemala, Nicaragua and Uruguay. In P. Merkle (ed.), *Political Violence and Terror*. Berkeley and Los Angeles: University of California Press.

Walker, J. (1992) *Violence and Conflict Resolution in Schools: A Study of the Teaching of Interpersonal Problem Solving Skills in Primary and Secondary Schools in Europe*. Brussels: Quaker Council for European Affairs.

Werth, J. L. and Lord, C. G. (1992) Previous conceptions of the typical group member and the contact hypothesis. *Banc and Applied Social Psychology*, 13, 3, 351–69.

Wetherell, M. and Potter, J. (1992) *Mapping the Language of Racism: Discourse and the Legitimation of Exploitation*. New York: Harvester Wheatsheaf.

Whyte, J. (1983) Control and supervision of urban 12-year-olds within and outside Northern Ireland: a pilot study. *Irish Journal of Psychology*, 6, 37–45.

Wilder, D. A. (1986) Social categorization: implications for creation of intergroup conflict. In L. Berkowitz (ed.), *Advances in Experimental Social Psychology*. New York: Academic Press.

Wilder, D. A. and Thompson, J. G. (1980) Intergroup contact with independent manipulations of intergroup and outgroup interaction. *Journal of Personality and Social Psychology*, 38, 589–603.

Wilson, J. P. and Raphael, B. (1993) *International Handbook of Traumatic Stress Syndromes*. New York: Plenum.

Wilson, R and Cairns, E. (1992) Troubles, stress and psychological disorder in Northern Ireland. *The Psychologist*, 5, 8, 347–50.

Wittkower, E. and Shellane, J. P. (1940) A survey of the literature of neuroses in war. In E. Miller (ed.), *The Neuroses in War*. London: Macmillan.

Woods, G. (1989) Rebels with a cause: the discontent of black youth. *Indicator South Africa*, 7, 1, 63–5.

Yogev, A., Ben-Yehoshua, N. S. and Alper, Y. (1991) Determinants of readiness for contact with Jewish children among young Arab students in Israel. *Journal of Conflict Resolution*, 35, 3, 547–62.

Yule, V. (1988) Some reflections on the cycle of violence in Northern Ireland and its impact on children. In E. J. Anthony and C. Chiland (eds), *The Child in his Family: Perilous Development: Child Rearing and Identity Formation Under Stress*. New York: Wiley.

Ziv, A. and Israel, R. (1973) Effects of bombardment on the manifest anxiety level of children living in kibbutzim. *Journal of Counselling and Clinical Psychology*, 40, 287–91.

Ziv, A. and Kruglanski, A. W. and Schulman, S. (1974) Children's psychological reactions to wartime stress. *Journal of Personality and Social Psychology*, 30, 24–30.

Index